COMING OFF TRANQUILLIZERS

Takes the reader through simple descriptions of the
meaning of dependence and the illness caused by
withdrawal, and provides detailed withdrawal plans.

My thanks to the members of the medical profession who have been patient and encouraging and also to Pat and the volunteers.

COMING OFF

TRANQUILLIZERS

AND SLEEPING PILLS

A Withdrawal Plan
That Really <u>Works</u>

by

Shirley Trickett SRN

Illustrated by Lucy Rickards

THORSONS PUBLISHING GROUP
Wellingborough, Northamptonshire
·
Rochester, Vermont

This edition first published June 1986
Second Impression December 1986
Third Impression June 1987

British Library Cataloguing in Publication Data

Trickett, Shirley
    Coming off tranquillizers: a withdrawal
    plan that really works.
    1. Benzodiazepine abuse—Treatment
    I. Title
    616.86'3   RC568.B4

ISBN 0-7225-1296-1

Printed and bound in Great Britain

CONTENTS

Note to reader

Before following the self-help advice given in this book readers are earnestly urged to give careful consideration to the nature of their particular health problem, and to consult a competent physician if in any doubt. This book should not be regarded as a substitute for professional medical treatment, and whilst every care is taken to ensure the accuracy of the content, the author and the publishers cannot accept legal responsibility for any problem arising out of the experimentation with the methods described.

FOREWORD

This book will become a 'bible' for thousands of men and women who, through no fault of their own, find themselves faced with the problems of benzodiazepine dependence and withdrawal. Many doctors have also turned to it for information and advice on the management of a syndrome still largely uncharted in the medical literature.

Shirley Trickett has done much to draw the attention of the medical profession and the public to the adverse effects of long-term benzodiazepine use and the difficulties of withdrawal. A trained nurse with an understanding of drugs and a talent for applying those skills which help people help themselves, she has greater experience than most doctors of the range of physical and psychological problems confronting those who wish to come off their tranquillizers. Her efforts led to the instigation of one of the country's earliest and most effective tranquillizer support groups, 'Come Off It' (1982), which has been the inspiration for similar groups in this country and abroad. Shirley Trickett's sound clinical judgement and practical advice have already proved invaluable to 500 clients in the North East. Doctors too have reason to be grateful to 'Come Off It' for providing their patients with the close personal contact, everyday support, and encouragement that many of them need.

This comprehensive book gives clear descriptions and straightforward explanations of the many symptoms which often bewilder patients undergoing withdrawal, as well as sensible, balanced advice on how to cope with them. Useful tables provide information on drug equivalents and suggested schemes for dosage reduction. Above all, the approach is optimistic with the constant reassurance that the sufferer *will* win through to recovery. Readers throughout the world will be glad of the insight and encouragement they will find in the following pages.

C.H. ASHTON, D.M., F.R.C.P.

Senior Lecturer in Psychopharmacology,
University of Newcastle upon Tyne;
Honorary Consultant in Clinical Pharmacology.

PREFACE

ALL WITHDRAWAL SYMPTOMS PASS IN TIME

This book has been written to give comfort and information to those suffering from the problems caused by tranquillizer withdrawal. It is hoped that it will be a practical guide for those who have not yet started to withdraw, and will also explain some of the strange symptoms experienced by those who have completed withdrawal.

Many of the symptoms are due to increased levels of anxiety due to drug withdrawal, and are not because you are 'silly', 'highly strung', neurotic, or 'unable to cope'. If you are well whilst you are taking tranquillizers and have no unpleasant symptoms when you stop taking them, you will not need this information.

Some medical terms have been included to help you understand them if you read them elsewhere.

When tranquillizers were first marketed over twenty years ago, doctors were told that they were safe and non-addictive. More recent research has disproved this. In the past few years, valiant efforts have been made by a few top scientists to change medical opinion, but it may take time for the correct information to be accepted by all doctors.

'Release', a London organization that deals mainly with people dependent on heroin, has done an enormous amount of work to help tranquillizer victims. They have compiled a national contact list of people who have coped with tranquillizer withdrawal, and are willing to support others. Their pamphlet 'Trouble with Tranquillizers' has given hope to thousands.

Withdrawal reactions vary enormously. Some people come off their pills without any problems at all, others have minor discomfort, but those who withdraw abruptly without guidance are the ones most likely to have problems.

It is hoped that as more doctors are educated in withdrawal management, and have more access to counsellors who offer alternative ways of coping with stress, the situation will dramatically improve.

Shirley Trickett, SRN
July 1986

INTRODUCTION

'Am I going mad?' 'Will I ever recover?' These are questions being asked by people experiencing symptoms of tranquillizer withdrawal all over the world. The reply from lay-counsellors (who have been through withdrawal) and from doctors who have knowledge of the problem is: 'No, you are not going mad', and 'Yes, you will recover, but it is going to take time.'

There is no doubt that tranquillizers help alleviate the distressing symptoms of anxiety. They do not make the problems go away, although they can help to keep you calm in times of stress. Some people tolerate them well and are able to discontinue them when they feel better. Unfortunately, many (about one quarter of users) are not so lucky. They can suffer from side-effects, withdrawal reactions, or both.

Few drugs have only the desired therapeutic action. People on tranquillizers often experience the following side-effects: depression, agoraphobia, loss of appetite, nausea, colic, diarrhoea, sinus pains, dizziness, confusion, outbursts of rage, lack of co-ordination, speech difficulties, change of personality, aches in joints and muscles and feeling emotionally dead.

1.

WHAT DEPENDENCE MEANS

When a substance that is not necessary for the normal functioning of the body is taken, for example, alcohol, cigarettes or caffeine, the body chemistry has to adjust to cope with the new substance. If the body comes to rely on the introduced chemical to function normally, this is dependence.

Tolerance is when more and more of the substance has to be taken to achieve the same effect, and withdrawal means reducing or stopping the new substance.

If a person becomes physically or nervously ill when they are deprived of the introduced chemical in sufficient amounts, these are the withdrawal symptoms.

Recovery Time

This is the length of time it takes to rid the body of the poisons, plus the time it takes for the body chemistry to return to normal.

Natural substances produced in the brain that help us cope with anxiety are 'knocked out' by the drugs. These have to be produced again before recovery can be complete.

Benzodiazepine (tranquillizer) dependence differs from heroin and alcohol addiction in that physical and not psychological dependence is the greater problem. Another difference is that it is prescribed medication and not self-poisoning. Pleasure-seeking behaviour as seen in other addictions is not evident in tranquillizer use. Many users are revolted by them, and feel angry that they have to take them to keep withdrawal symptoms at bay.

How Long Will It Take?

Planning withdrawal

Everyone asks this and there is no simply reply. For some it takes weeks, others months, but it may be up to two years before all the symptoms have completely gone. That does not mean that you are going to feel ill all that time, but that a few persistent symptoms may linger.

You may feel less able to cope with stress for six months or more after withdrawal. It is important to realize that this state will not be permanent. Some people go back on their pills at this stage thinking there will be no further improvement.

If during the recovery time you have a serious crisis in your life it may be necessary to take an anti-anxiety drug for a short time (preferably not the one from which you have withdrawn). Many have done this and have still successfully completed withdrawal when life has settled down.

Your positive attitude towards withdrawal and taking care of your general health can speed up recovery. Some people carry on with their work all during withdrawal.

Why Should I Come Off My Pills?

If you stay on tranquillizers for long periods, even if you are not dependent, here are some of the risks you run:

Depression

Some doctors argue that the reason for the depressing effect of tranquillizers is that when anxiety is controlled underlying depression manifests itself. This does not explain why some people who have neither anxiety or depression before drugs, become depressed when they take them.

Change of Personality

Relatives often complain that the user has become 'moody', irritable and distant. After withdrawal many users have said, 'Now that I feel myself again I realize how different my personality was when I was on the pills'.

Chronic Vague Ill Health

This is common particularly in long-term users. They complain of lethargy, digestive upsets, and pains and aches. They often look the same too. The hair is lank, the eyes glazed and the complexion is pale or a light muddy colour.

Increased Risk of Accident

Statistics show clearly that there is an increased risk of accident on the road, operating machinery, and in the home, during benzodiazepine therapy. This may be because of lack of co-ordination, loss of concentration and memory lapses.

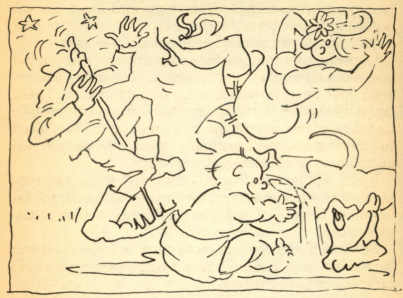

The Illness Caused by Tranquillizer Withdrawal

This can be severe if a careful reduction plan is not followed. So many people throw their pills down the lavatory when they realize they are dependent. They then have to rush off to the doctor for more when they cannot cope with the withdrawal symptoms. This is not because they lack willpower, nor because they imagine they need the support of the drugs, it is because they are *chemically* dependent.

If a steady reduction plan is followed, the symptoms will be much less severe. The aim is to avoid sudden drops in the level of the drug in the blood. This is when the symptoms are at their worst. Slow withdrawal is safe. Whilst there still may be some discomfort, and you may get impatient, the results will be worth your efforts.

The symptoms mentioned on pages 28 to 75 are mainly

the experiences of people who have tried to reduce too quickly without medical help. If you understand what is temporarily happening to your body and mind, you will not get so anxious about withdrawal. The support of your doctor and family is most important at this time.

Dependence on any substance can be degrading, but you must remember that this is a therapeutic dependence, and therefore you should not feel ashamed. These drugs were given to you as a medicine. Suppose penicillin had dependence-producing properties, and it was given to you for some life-threatening disease. Would you feel guilty about the resulting dependence?

It is a sad fact that many people feel guilty, not only about their dependence on the drugs, but also about the nervous illness for which the drug was originally prescribed.

Some of the 'addicts' do not have a history of nervous illness. It may be they were prescribed for a temporary life problem, or back injury, and were then given years of un-queried repeat prescriptions. So many times a tearful person will say, 'What can I do? I feel confused and emotionally dead on the pills, but I am afraid to stop them in case my original illness comes back.' The truth is that if the drugs have been taken continuously for more than 3–4 months, they may be having very little therapeutic effect on the original symptoms. The user may only be avoiding withdrawal symptoms by continuing medication, and still suffer the toxic effects of the drugs into the bargain!

Understanding Withdrawal

This could take most of the fear of the illness away, and hasten your recovery. *You will recover*—but there may be times when you need to be constantly reassured about this. Talking with someone who has been through withdrawal, or a sympathetic doctor, is the first step on the road to recovery. Try to overcome feelings of guilt, or of being a nuisance. It often only takes a two-minute telephone call to allay a fear, or explain a symptom. As you recover, your confidence will grow, and as you become more independent, reliance on your helper will disappear.

How Do I Know if I Am Dependent on Tranquillizers?

If you feel that the pills have stopped working and you have to increase the dose to get the same effect, or if you feel ill when you do not take the pills, then you could be dependent.

What to Do if You Feel You Are Dependent on Tranquillizers

If you are in the 'Catch 22' situation of feeling ill whilst you are taking the pills; worse when you stop; and have symptoms of increased anxiety and depression, panic attacks, sweating, insomnia—see your doctor.

You will need the doctor's advice before reducing your pills. Tranquillizers are also used for conditions other than nervous illness. You may need an alternative prescription.

It may be that your doctor has a good knowledge of withdrawal procedure, and is sympathetic and willing to guide you through. If this is not the case, and he refuses to believe how ill you feel, or is hostile because he feels you are trying to tell him his job, seek help from a support group. These are run nation-wide, usually by ex-users who have a great deal of experience because of the enormous numbers of people coming for help. All you need is your doctor's approval to come off, and then you can refer to your nearest group. They will help you to work out a slow withdrawal programme that can be carried out at home.

The Elderly and Tranquillizers or Sleeping Pills

Complete withdrawal in the elderly dependent person is often inadvisable, although it may be necessary to reduce the dose slowly until the side-effects (toxic confusion and loss of balance) are minimized.

Write to the following addresses for your nearest contact:

Tranx   MIND
17 Peel Road   22 Harley Street
Harrow   London W1
Middlesex HA3 7QX

or telephone your nearest MIND group.

For 'Trouble with Tranquillizers' send 80p + 20p postage to:

RELEASE
1–4 Hatton Place
Hatton Gardens
London EC1N 8ND

Remember: It is dangerous to stop your drugs abruptly. Acute withdrawal should only be carried out in hospital.

2.

HOW DO I COME OFF MY PILLS?

The speed at which you can withdraw may depend on what is happening in your life. If you have a stressful job, particularly where driving or operating machinery is involved, or have young children or a sick person depending on you, it may have to be taken slowly.

Acute Withdrawal in Hospital

If sick leave is possible, your doctor may be able to arrange hospital admission. This is usually advisable after a long drug history, or where the side-effects are causing chronic ill health. A four to six week stay is usual with at least two weeks without the drugs before leaving hospital. For some, there will still be a recovery period after discharge.

Since this is essentially a medical problem, a pharmacological or drug dependence unit is preferable. Some people refuse a bed in a psychiatric hospital. Others are eager to come off their drugs quickly and will go anywhere. Resist well-meaning therapists who attempt psychological probing in early withdrawal. You may not have deep psychological problems. Even if you have, it is not the time for the 'Why do you hate your father?' approach. It should be a time for rest and reassurance. Deep conflicts will arise spontaneously if they need to.

Try not to develop a 'pill phobia'. Accepting other

drugs temporarily to keep you comfortable could help your recovery.

It is exciting to see the physical changes that appear as people come off their tranquillizers—eyes lose the dull glazed look, skin colour and texture improve, and hair comes back to life.

Slow Withdrawal

Many people withdraw very successfully at home. If your doctor has agreed that you should reduce, but has not given you a withdrawal regime, here are some suggestions:

The Open University course called 'Anxiety and Benzodiazepines (Tranquillizers)' recommends a dose reduction of $\frac{1}{8}$th of the daily dose per 2–4 weeks. Some people feel that this regime prolongs the agony and prefer to tolerate symptoms of a more rapid withdrawal. The course also recommends that where a short-acting drug (e.g. Ativan) is being taken, a long-acting drug (e.g. Valium) be substituted. This can be done when the lowest possible dose of the short-acting drug is reached. Alternatively the recommendation for Diazepam (Valium) substitution from the Drugs Newsletter, No. 31, April, 1985, of the Regional Drug Information Service, Newcastle upon Tyne, can be used.

> The benzodiazepine in use should be replaced in increments of one dose per day by the equivalent dose of diazepam [see Appendix]. This substitution can usually be accomplished within a week, although the duration of this period should be varied to suit individual patients. For example, a regime for a patient taking Lorazepam 1mg morning, midday and evening is to replace the evening dose with 10mg Diazepam for two days, then add replacement of the midday dose for two days, and finally replace the morning dose. The patient is then taking a daily dose of 30 mg Diazepam, which is approximately equivalent to 3 mg Lorazepam. Some patients feel better when Lorazepam or other relatively short-acting benzodiazepines are replaced by Diazepam in this manner. Some, however, require slightly more than the approximately equivalent dose of Diazepam given in the table to replace the benzodiazepine they are used to. A minority of patients experience real difficulties in changing from one benzodiazepine to another. In these cases, the changeover needs to be carried out more gradually.

It is generally agreed that the short-acting drugs cause most problems during withdrawal.

Many people have found the short-term or intermittent use of Propranolol (Inderal) useful. It helps the panic attacks, palpitations, sweating, and is a mild sedative.

This book is concerned only with minor tranquillizers (Benzodiazepines).

It is extremely important to check with your doctor before you reduce any drugs.

Do not compare the numbers of milligrammes—1 mg of one drug cannot be substituted for 1 mg of another drug. 5 mg of Ativan does not equal 5 mg of Valium or 5 mg of Mogadon.

Points in Favour of Slow Withdrawal

1. Symptoms are less severe.
2. Better if you have a stressful job or domestic life.
3. Better for long-term users if hospitalization is not possible.
4. Gives time to adjust to deep emotional problems (if they exist).
5. General health can be improved at the same time, and therefore make withdrawal easier.
6. May be the best way for the person who has always been severely anxious.
7. Reduces risk of going back on pills.

SLOW WITHDRAWAL TABLES

These are only a guide. Where they show unequal dosage work out which part of the day you need the higher dose. Unless you are accustomed to only one dose per day, divide the daily dose as evenly as possible. By doing this you will avoid sudden drops of the level of the drug in the blood.

ATIVAN (LORAZEPAM)

Some doctors prefer to change their patients from Ativan to Valium, then withdraw the Valium—10 mg Valium are substituted for 1 mg Ativan. Others prefer their patients to cut down their Ativan as far as they can, and then change over to Valium for the last part of withdrawal. If side-effects are a problem it is sensible to change over at the beginning.

If you are on 6–8 mg Ativan you may be able to cut down to half the dose quite quickly, giving up 1 mg per 1 to 2 weeks and then proceed with slow withdrawal for the rest.

Ativan tablets are difficult to cut into small doses. Some chemists are willing to make up ¼ mg doses into capsules.

Some people prefer to dissolve ½ mg Ativan in 10 ml of water, then divide it into 2 × 5 ml doses. Plastic 5 ml spoons are available from chemists.

ATIVAN (LORAZEPAM) 1 mg Tablets

Name of Drug Ativan	Daily Dose	Morning	Lunchtime	Evening
If you are on	3 tabs. (3 mg)	1 tab.	1 tab.	1 tab.
Cut down to	2½ tabs.	1 tab.	½ tab.	1 tab.
2 to 4 weeks later cut down to	2 tabs.	1 tab.	½ tab.	½ tab.
4 weeks later cut down to	1½ tabs.	½ tab.	½ tab.	½ tab.
cut down to	1¼ tabs.	½ tab.	¼ tab.	½ tab.
cut down to	1 tab.	½ tab.	¼ tab.	¼ tab.
cut down to	¾ tab.	¼ tab.	¼ tab.	¼ tab.
6 weeks later cut down to	⅜ tab.	⅛ tab.	⅛ tab.	⅛ tab.
cut down to	¼ tab.	⅛ tab.	—	⅛ tab.
cut down to	⅛ tab.	Take this ⅛ tab. when you need it most.		

VALIUM (DIAZEPAM) 2 mg TABLETS

Name of Drug Valium	Daily Dose	Morning	Lunchtime	Evening
If you are on	7½ tabs. (15 mg)	2½ tabs.	2½ tabs.	2½ tabs.
Cut down to	5½ tabs.	2 tabs.	1½ tabs.	2 tabs.
2 to 4 weeks later				
cut down to	4 tabs.	1¼ tabs.	1¼ tabs.	1½ tabs.
cut down to	3 tabs.	1 tab.	1 tab.	1 tab.
cut down to	2½ tabs.	¾ tab.	¾ tab.	¾ tab.
cut down to	1¾ tabs.	½ tab.	½ tab.	¾ tab.
cut down to	1¼ tabs.	½ tab.	¼ tab.	½ tab.
cut down to	¾ tab.	¼ tab.	¼ tab.	¼ tab.
cut down to	½ tab.	⅛ tab.	⅛ tab.	¼ tab.
cut down to	¼ tab.	⅛ tab.	—	⅛ tab.
cut down to	⅛ tab.	⅛ tab.	—	—

Librium (Chlordiazepoxide)

Some capsules can be taken apart and fitted together again. If not, ask the doctor to prescribe empty capsules. Divide powder and put it into empty capsule.

Some powders are irritants. Avoid taking powder without capsule. When 2½ mg (½ capsule) daily dose is reached, you may wish to ask your doctor to substitute an equivalent amount of Valium. It will be easier to complete withdrawal by cutting up tablets rather than dividing tiny amounts of powder.

LIBRIUM 5 mg CAPSULES

Name of Drug Librium	Daily Dose	Morning	Lunchtime	Evening
If you are on	3 caps. (15 mg)	1 cap.	1 cap.	1 cap.

Name of Drug	Daily Dose	Morning	Lunchtime	Evening
Cut down to	2½ caps.	1 cap.	½ cap.	1 cap.
2–4 weeks later				
cut down to	2 caps.	½ cap.	½ cap.	1 cap.
cut down to	1½ caps.	½ cap.	½ cap.	½ cap.
cut down to	1 cap.	½ cap.	—	½ cap.
4–6 weeks later				
cut down to	½ cap.	—	—	½ cap.

Mogadon (Nitrazepam)

Accept that, for a time, the sleeping pattern may be disturbed. This is a positive sign. It shows that your body is getting rid of the toxins.

MOGADON 5 mg TABLETS

Name of Drug Mogadon	Nightly Dose
If you are on	2 tablets
Cut down to	1½ tablets
4–6 weeks later	
cut down to	1 tablet
cut down to	¾ tablet
cut down to	½ tablet
cut down to	¼ tablet
cut down to	⅛ tablet

Rapid Withdrawal

If you are impatient to be drug-free, and particularly if you are fit and not a very long-term user, you may wish to use Professor Lader's 4 or 6 week rapid withdrawal plan.

There are many views on how best to withdraw. Discuss with your doctor which way would be best for you.

Points in Favour of Rapid Withdrawal:

1. A drug-free state is reached earlier.

2. There is psychological benefit from not having to swallow an abhorrent substance any longer than necessary.
3. Best method for impatient people.
4. Best method for short-term users.

Here is an example of Professor Malcolm Lader's recommendations.

It is not safe to withdraw faster than this.

RAPID WITHDRAWAL TABLE

VALIUM (DIAZEPAM) 15 mg (2 mg tablets)

Week No.	Morning	Lunchtime	Evening	Total	
1.	2 tabs.	2 tabs.	2 tabs.	6 tabs.	= 12 mg
2.	1½ tabs.	1½ tabs.	1½ tabs.	4½ tabs.	= 9 mg
3.	1 tab.	1 tab.	1 tab.	3 tabs.	= 6 mg
4.	½ tab.	½ tab.	½ tab.	1½ tabs.	= 3 mg

For a dose of 30 mg Valium daily, six weeks is the minimum withdrawal period. If this method is too quick to tolerate, change to a slower one.

And for my next trick . . .

3.

WITHDRAWAL SYMPTOMS

If you consider what the drugs do, i.e. control anxiety, relax nerves and muscles, help you sleep, and slow down heartbeats and breathing, it is understandable that your body will complain loudly when they are cut down or stopped.

The opposite of the desired effect can be expected (in some people) for a time. This is called the rebound reaction.

Do not be alarmed by this list of symptoms. You may only experience a couple of them, particularly if you reduce carefully:

increased anxiety, increased depression: insomnia: panic attacks: suicidal feelings: agoraphobia: outbursts of rage: flu-like symptoms: hyperactivity: craving for tablets: hallucinations (seeing and hearing things): confusion: headaches: dizziness: sweating: palpitations: slow pulse: tight chest: abdominal pain: nausea: nightmares: restlessness: increased sensitivity to light, noise, touch and smell: sore eyes: blurred vision: creeping sensation in the skin, loss of interest in sex: impotence: pain in jaw or face: sore tongue: metallic taste: pain in the shoulders and neck: sore heavy limbs: pins and needles: jelly legs: shaking. Fits have been reported but *only* where drugs have been stopped abruptly.

Remember that some people don't get *any* of the above

symptoms and also that there is now much more help than in previous years for those who do have discomfort.

Why some people become physically dependent on tranquillizers (or any other substance), and others don't is unknown. It is possible that people who become addicted to benzodiazepines are those who are also allergic to them. Dr Richard Mackarness, in his book *A Little of What You Fancy,* describes masked allergies in alcohol and cigarette dependence. When even small doses of the substance are taken the masked allergy is under control. There are certainly many allergic-type symptoms in withdrawal, and they appear after complete withdrawal.

All Withdrawal Symptoms Pass in Time

Accepting withdrawal symptoms as part of getting well could shorten your recovery time. Try to see a new symptom as a positive step nearer to a drug-free life.

You are working towards a state of physical and mental well-being that you may not have experienced for years. You may have been emotionally dead for so long, unable to respond normally to pleasure or pain. So even if you are uncomfortable in withdrawal, you will be coming alive again and will have glimpses, even in the early days, of a world you thought you had forgotten.

Anxiety

Most of the withdrawal symptoms are due to manifestations of anxiety. This does not mean simply worrying about the weather or which dress to wear for a party, but disabling physical and emotional symptoms which prevent the sufferer from leading a normal life. Clinical tests have proved that anxiety levels after the drugs have been discontinued can be six times greater than

pre-withdrawal levels. This is called rebound anxiety.

Tranquillizers appear to stop that part of the brain that deals with anxiety from working—but this is not really so. It carries on working overtime under the 'lid' of the drugs, and consequently when the 'lid' is removed, it erupts like a volcano. This is temporary, *and will return to normal*.

It will take time for the body's normal chemicals to be produced again. When you understand that there is a definite physiological reason why you may feel more anxious during withdrawal, this will give you the confidence to ignore the 'pull yourself together' brigade. This point is also illustrated by the large numbers of people who are prescribed these drugs for a physical reason who also have anxiety symptoms on withdrawal.

When you have a major problem or upset in life, it is often necessary to relieve anxiety for a short time, but it is a great mistake to carry on for months or years. Not only does the user run the risk of dependence, but also because the emotions are dulled, he or she is unable to adjust to the loss or altered situation. This is particularly so in bereavement. The user has to face the grief again when medication ceases, and may feel severe guilt about not grieving at the appropriate time. Because the suppressed emotions of years come to the surface in withdrawal, many people are able to face old conflicts and traumas, and in doing so, lose some of their fears, and gain self-respect.

To illustrate how many (although it is agreed not all) of the withdrawal symptoms are due to rebound anxiety, here are anxiety symptoms listed under 'Anxiety Neurosis' from the *Oxford Textbook of Psychiatry* (1983), Ed. Gelder, Gath and Mayou. Some people have found this section rather technical, others were finally convinced (because the source was beyond dispute) that they were not suffering from some serious physical illness.

Anxiety neuroses have psychological and physical symptoms. The psychological symptoms are the familiar feeling of fearful anticipation that gives the condition its name, irritability, difficulty in concentration, sensitivity to noise, and a feeling of restlessness.

Patients often complain of poor memory when they are really experiencing the effects of failure to concentrate.

Repetitive thoughts form an important part of an anxiety neurosis. These are often provoked by awareness of autonomic over-activity; e.g. a patient who feels his heart beating fast may worry about having a heart attack. Thoughts of this kind probably prolong the condition.

The appearance of a person with an anxiety neurosis is characteristic. His or her face looks strained, with a furrowed brow; the posture is tense; he or she is restless and often tremulous. The skin looks pale, and sweating is common especially from the hands, feet and axillae (armpits).

Readiness to tears, which may at first suggest depression, reflects a generally apprehensive state.

The physical symptoms and signs of an anxiety neurosis result from either over-activity in the sympathetic nervous system or increased tension in skeletal muscles.

The list of symptoms is long, and is conveniently grouped by systems of the body. Symptoms related to the gastro-intestinal tract include dry mouth, difficulty in swallowing, epigastric discomfort (under breastbone), excessive wind caused by aerophagy (air swallowing), borborygmi (rumbling of intestinal gases), and frequent or loose motions.

Common respiratory symptoms, include a feeling of constriction in the chest, difficulty in inhaling (which contrasts with the expiratory difficulty in asthma), and over-breathing and its consequences (which are described later).

Cardiovascular symptoms include palpitations, a feeling of discomfort or pain over the heart, awareness of missed beats, and throbbing in the neck.

Common genito-urinary symptoms are increased frequency and urgency of micturition (act of passing urine), failure of erection, and lack of libido.

Women may complain of increased menstrual discomfort and sometimes amenorrhoea (absence of menstruation).

Complaints related to the functions of the central nervous system include tinnitus, blurring of vision, prickling sensations, and dizziness (which is not rotational).

Other symptoms may be related to muscular tension. In the scalp this may be experienced as aching or stiffness, especially in the back and shoulders. The hands may tremble so that delicate movements are impaired.

In anxiety neuroses sleep is disturbed in a characteristic way. On going to bed, the patient lies awake worrying; when at last he falls asleep, he wakes intermittently. He often reports unpleasant dreams.

Stress

We all have a part of the brain that works to keep us normally restless and anxious at an acceptable level. During stress and illness, this mechanism may become over-stimulated, so we become over-anxious.

The body reacts to the chemicals poured into the bloodstream, and this gives us the distressing physical feelings which we associate with anxiety: heart beating wildly, stomach churning, shaking and sweating.

If your arm was injured and needed rest, you would put it in a sling. You can learn to give your exhausted nervous system the same kind of comfort and rest.

Dr Claire Weekes gives excellent advice in her books and tapes. In *Self-help For Your Nerves*, she asks you to accept your nervous illness, float through, and not fight against the physical symptoms and let time pass. This may sound difficult, particularly if you are coping with misery in your life. However, her advice is sound. If you fight your symptoms, you will further stimulate your over-sensitized nerves, and end up even more exhausted and ill. Accepting your fear may be the hardest thing you have ever done, but think of the rewards.

If you have a weak chest, catching a chill, or getting over-tired, could result in bronchitis. In the same way, if your nerves are over-strained, an unexpected gas bill or even a door banging may make you feel ill.

Depersonalization

This can happen when anxiety levels are high. People who have never had drugs can also suffer this. Perhaps this is the main symptom that induces feelings of going mad. People feel they are not real, not in touch with themselves, and worry that their mental processes are going to break down completely. 'I look in the mirror I know it's me, but it does not look like me—I don't really recognize my image.'

It could be that the anxiety feelings are too much for you to cope with so you retreat (although not consciously) to 'not being you'. If this is very severe the sufferer may hallucinate, 'seeing' themselves or their faces. As anxiety decreases the feelings and hallucinations completely disappear.

De-Realization

This means not feeling in touch with reality, and feeling

strange in familiar surroundings. People say 'I walk into my kitchen and it does not look like my kitchen'. Some people say 'How can it be anxiety. I am happy about cutting down my pills, and there is nothing in my life to make me anxious'. Even if this is so, your body (and therefore your mind) may still be in a state of stress because of withdrawal. Learn to relax and these feelings will disappear.

Lack of Concentration

Calls come in saying 'How is it that I am having difficulty doing simple things I have done all my life?' One said 'It has taken me two hours to fit a plug onto a kettle'. Many women have said that they could not understand the simplest recipe or knitting pattern.

There is some confusion between memory lapses and loss of concentration. Many people have said that they make appointments and then forget them. It may be that

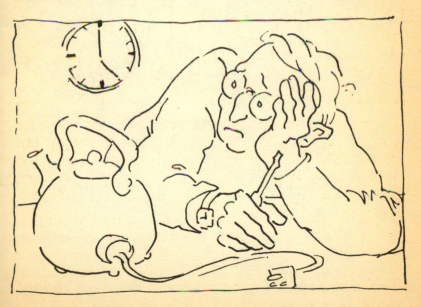

because of lack of concentration at the time, they have failed to take in the information rather than subsequently forgetting it. Concentration does improve as withdrawal progresses. Life can be very boring when you cannot concentrate on reading or watching television. Large print books (helpful if you have sore eyes) are available from most libraries. You may need to choose 'light' reading material for a while. Some people stimulate concentration by doing simple crossword puzzles.

Loss of Memory

When users become aware again after years of emotional hibernation, they realize that they have no recollection, or only vague impressions of significant events in their lives. One woman said 'My grandson is now eleven, he has always lived in my house, and since I have come off pills, my thinking is clearer, but I cannot remember his birth or his growing up'. This experience is typical.

Some people have said that they have gone back to the emotional state they were in when they first took drugs. One man in his thirties who was first prescribed tranquillizers when he was seventeen said he felt adolescent again when he was drug-free.

Panic Attacks

These can cause a great deal of distress during withdrawal. The sufferer is suddenly overwhelmed by fear for no apparent reason, and often feels that death is not far away. Some feel unable to move or speak, others shout out for help. Although the attacks usually last only a few minutes it can seem much longer to the sufferer.

In a person who is not nervously ill, an exam, or even an exciting social event may produce 'butterflies in the stomach'; sweating hands; constriction of the chest; a rise in the heart rate, etc. This is a normal response. A panic attack is an exaggeration of this, due to an exhausted nervous system. If you are over-enthusiastic the first time you go out jogging, your muscles will complain the next day, by being stiff and sore. Panic attacks, agoraphobia, irritability, and many other symptoms are a similar cry for help from your nervous system. It is saying 'Do not abuse me, I have had enough'.

It is often hard to convince someone who is having panic attacks that it is not the onset of some terrible disease. Every symptom—wildly beating heart; rapid breathing; sweating; shaking—is part of the 'fright and flight' response. We would be lost without it. We do not want to stop it, but to get it back to normal.

Primitive man needed to be able to react like this to escape from dangerous animals. We may need it now to get out of the path of the number 33 bus, or a youth on a skateboard! Fear stimulates the chemicals that make us respond quickly. That unpleasant sinking feeling in the

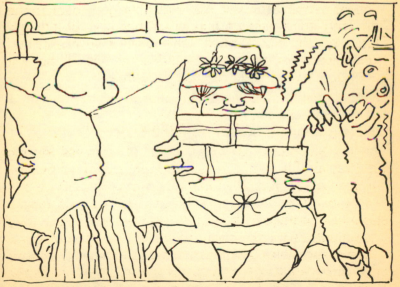

You can learn to control panic anywhere

abdomen is only a sudden diversion of blood away from internal organs to the legs to make them move faster.

The following article shows that severe symptoms including panic attacks can arise from simply not breathing correctly.

'Hyperventilation [shallow breathing] as a Cause of Panic Attacks', Dr Hibbert, *British Medical Journal*, Vol. 288, 28.1.84.

The syndrome [collection of symptoms] characterized by repeated panic attacks has been known by several names, including muscular exhaustion of the heart, neurasthenia (nervous exhaustion), irritable heart, anxiety neurosis, effort syndrome, and cardiac neurosis. The manual's definition of panic disorder states that attacks are manifested by the sudden onset of intense apprehension, fear, or terror, often associated with feelings of impending doom. The most common symptoms experienced during an attack are dyspnoea (difficult breathing), palpitations, chest pain or discomfort, choking or smothering sensations, dizziness, vertigo, or unsteady feelings, feelings of unreality, paraesthesias (disordered sensation such as tingling and pins and needles) hot and cold flushes, sweating, faintness, trembling or shaking and fear of dying, going crazy or doing something uncontrolled during the attack. Attacks usually last minutes; more rarely hours.

Remember it is essential to breathe slowly if you feel a panic attack coming on.

Here is another extract from the *Oxford Textbook of Psychiatry* (1983):

This shows again the importance of attention to correct breathing. Over-breathing is breathing in a rapid and shallow way which results in a fall in the concentration of carbon dioxide in the blood. The resultant symptoms include dizziness, tinnitus (noises in the ears), headache, a feeling of weakness, faintness, numbness and tingling in the hands, feet, and face, carpopedal spasms (severe cramp in hands and feet), and precordial discomfort (area of the chest over the heart). There is also a feeling of breathlessness which may prolong the condition. When a patient has unexplained bodily symptoms, the possibility of persistent overbreathing should always be borne in mind.

The anxious person tends to overbreathe, whilst the depressed person often takes a short in-breath and has a long sighing out-breath.

How to Cope with Panic Attacks

If your attitude is 'I will die, be sick, faint, wet my pants, etc., if I don't fight this panic attack', you will encourage more attacks. It will become a trigger for stimulating more hormones and more fear. If you teach your body to give the correct messages to your brain, you can break this chain reaction.

When an attack comes, breathe out long and hard, and pause before you breathe in. Dr Hibbert suggests putting a cold wet cloth on the cheeks. This acts on the diving reflex and slows down the breathing very effectively. If you slow down your breathing (by breathing from the abdomen) it will be impossible for symptoms to become worse. Abdominal breathing is allowing full lung expansion by raising the abdomen on the in-breath.

Cupping the hands or hold a *paper* (not plastic) bag over the nose and mouth whilst breathing normally will increase carbon dioxide levels and help to calm you within a few minutes.

Try not to be embarrassed about letting those around you know what is wrong. One young woman who shouts for help during attacks has learnt to explain that she is suffering from drug withdrawal symptoms, and that it will pass in a minute.

Dr Weekes's book was not written for people coming off drugs, but the illness she describes, which many would think of as a nervous breakdown, is very similar—a chemical nervous breakdown if you like. Some people are afraid of the words 'nervous breakdown'. It really means exhausted nerves. You will recover, no matter how long you have been ill, if you alter your attitude from 'I feel so bad I will never get better' to 'I know I will get better if I accept the illness, help my body to cope with it, and wait for time to heal'.

Hyperventilation (Over-breathing)

Clients find it very hard to believe that so many symptoms can be due simply to not breathing properly. Rapid, shallow breathing is very common in withdrawal. It may be due to spasm (tension) in respiratory muscles, or it may be that the central mechanism in the brain is temporarily disturbed. This does not mean that you will stop breathing, but it does mean you will have to practise abdominal breathing.

When someone is anxious, over-breathing is usually present (again part of the 'fright and flight' response), but in withdrawal it seems different. Users in hospital for acute withdrawal have been observed to over-breathe even whilst asleep.

Abdominal Breathing

Many users find this tedious, but when you look at the list of symptoms that can be due entirely to over-breathing, it could be worth the effort.

Tie something around your wrist to remind you to be aware of your breathing patterns.

1. Do two ½ hour breathing exercise sessions per day and note your breathing rate every hour.
2. Loosen anything tight around your waist and preferably lie on the bed or floor.
3. Allow your lungs to inflate fully by gently lifting your tummy out as you breathe in (it could make you a

little light-headed or tingly at first) and allow it to fall as you breathe out.
4. Try to keep the breaths equal and aim to gradually train yourself to breathe between 8 to 12 breaths per minute.
5. Don't exhaust yourself by doing this too vigorously. Once you have mastered this, you will be able to do it anywhere—standing at the bus stop; whilst ironing; whilst washing up.

Blood Sugar Levels in Withdrawal

It may be that the drugs artificially raise the blood sugar levels and therefore low blood sugar (hypoglycaemia) could be expected on withdrawal. Even if this is not so hypoglycaemic symptoms are often present in anxious people. The condition is not serious and is easily controlled by a sensible eating plan. Many have said that some of the withdrawal symptoms, e.g. shaking inside, confusion, and panic attacks improve if they do not allow themselves to get very hungry. You will see from the diet that sugar is not the answer to hypoglycaemia but it can be used as an emergency measure until a meal is possible. Carry glucose tablets, chocolate or sweets, particularly if you are driving or in any situation that needs concentration.

The following diet is an example of an eating plan that helps to keep the blood sugar stable. It is only a guide and not something to become over-anxious about. Many have found it greatly reduces the craving for sugar, or the desire for odd foods.

Suggested Diet for Tranquillizer Withdrawal

The main principles of the diet are:
Avoid or cut down on all quickly absorbed carbohydrate

including sugar, chocolate, sweets, white bread, white flour, cakes, biscuits, pastry, alcohol, soft drinks and anything with added sugar. Man's natural diet did not include these—you would be better off without them.

Reduce the intake of animal fat. Vegetable oils (corn or sunflower seed oil) may be used.

Eat wholemeal bread, wholegrain cereal, vegetables and fruit. Protein should be eaten at every meal. This can be lean meat, poultry, dairy produce, pulses, peas, beans, nuts and seeds.

Five or six small meals should be taken at regular intervals. Eat before going to bed, and as early as possible in the morning, to cut down the fasting time.

As soon as you get up:	small glass of unsweetened fruit juice/half a grapefruit/medium orange.
Breakfast:	more fruit juice or fruit. Choose from: Egg / bacon / kidney / baked beans/black pudding/kippers (or any fish)/cheese/cottage cheese/yogurt. Also wholemeal bread or toast with butter. Milk or weak tea without sugar.
Two hours after breakfast:	small glass of fruit juice, milk or yogurt.
Lunch:	Choose from: any cold or hot lean meat/chicken/fish (fresh or tinned), sardines, tuna, etc., salads/vegetables. Wholemeal bread or crispbread if desired.

Three hours after lunch: small glass milk/tea with crisp-
bread/yogurt
One hour before dinner: small glass fruit juice.
Dinner: same as lunch plus fruit.
Supper: crispbread with cheese, meat
paste, cottage cheese, etc.
Milk drink or weak tea.

If you are hungry between meals, eat a handful of unsalted nuts.

If you are overweight eat smaller quantities, but regularly.

Don't try this diet for just a few days then revert to your sugar-laden diet—try it for several weeks—many have found it very helpful.

Digestive problems are common in withdrawal. If you cannot manage the diet because you feel sick, or have diarrhoea, try to eat steamed fish, minced liver/chicken/meat or high protein baby food. To increase protein intake have *Sanatogen* powder or *Complan* in milk several times a day and particularly before bed. Vegetables will be easier to digest if sieved or liquidized.

Remember to eat often and avoid sugar and fat.

Note: Vegetarians can substitute all vegetable protein.

Caffeine in Withdrawal

Most people cut down on coffee, tea and coke because they realize their withdrawal symptoms are much worse after taking them.

Cigarettes in Withdrawal

Some people stop smoking completely because of the metallic taste in the mouth. Others smoke com-pulsively. You will feel better if you try to cut them down.

Alcohol in Withdrawal

On the whole, users say alcohol increases the withdrawal symptoms, although a few have said they have found it helpful for getting off to sleep. This should always be regarded as a short-term help because of the danger of substitution of one dependence-producing drug for another.

Insomnia

The rebound insomnia experienced in withdrawal can be severe. Your normal sleeping pattern may not return for weeks or months. Try to accept this. It will come back in time.

Even people who are well and not on drugs can have disturbing symptoms, e.g. depersonalization (not being in touch with themselves), and de-realization (not being in touch with reality), when they are deprived of sleep.

If you feel that the lack of sleep is seriously holding you back, your doctor may prescribe a sedative (just to give you a rest) for a short time. Check to make sure that it is not in the benzodiazepine group—i.e. Valium, Librium, Ativan, etc. (See tables on pages 100-104).

The dreams and nightmares that you are flooded with during withdrawal are just your mind doing work that it should have done months or years before.

The dreams are often described as evil. They include: violence; disaster; disturbed sexual behaviour. People who are distressed by incestuous or homosexual dreams feel greatly comforted when they learn it is a common experience in withdrawal, and will soon pass.

Recounting your dreams or writing them down when you wake sometimes helps to make you less anxious about them. Trust your mind to do the work. Your normal dreaming and sleeping pattern will return.

Those who suffer withdrawal insomnia say it is the most difficult symptom to cope with. So often it is said 'If only I could get a good night's sleep, I could cope with the days'. Sleeping only a couple of hours a night in early withdrawal is not uncommon. Although it is very hard to bear, try not to become too anxious about it. Withdrawal insomnia is a particularly severe form of insomnia—time is the only cure.

Lying in warm water or in a warm bed can give your muscles the rest they need. Listen to relaxation tapes, and practise abdominal breathing. Try to quieten your racing thoughts by concentrating on feeling the breath entering and leaving one nostril. Every time your concentration wanders away to your jumbled thoughts, just gently bring it back again to concentrating on your breath. Do not get angry with yourself for not even being able to do this simple task, just keep going for five minutes, then try later. This simple meditation is helpful if you can discipline yourself to do it regularly. Some people have found a radio with headphones very helpful; it cuts out external sound and helps to slow down racing thoughts.

Hyperactivity

The aimless hyperactivity experienced by some can be

very hard to live with. The constant desire to move is exhausting. Unfortunately, the energy cannot be utilized. The sufferer usually wanders about doing a small part of one task, then another without achieving anything. One caller said 'I wash two plates, then find myself putting laundry away upstairs. Two minutes later I am sweeping up leaves in the garden. My mind won't let me use the extra energy I have had since cutting down my pills'.

Pressure of thought and speech often accompany this stage. Endless conversations (sometimes from years before) or the same song can go around and around in your head.

Relatives often complain that the user has become completely self-centred, talking incessantly about the drugs and withdrawal symptoms. The sufferer is usually very anxious about these symptoms, and may need constant reassurance that they will pass.

Depression

You may feel delighted that you have managed to cut down or stop taking your pills, but be puzzled by how down you feel. This is another temporary state to endure. It will improve or disappear altogether when you are through withdrawal. Many people who have loving families and no financial worries, or stress of any kind, feel guilty about being so down.

Withdrawal blues do not single out people with life problems, many people have a temporary 'down'. Sometimes the depressive symptoms are delayed and appear when the sufferers feel they are coping well. Try not to get discouraged if this happens—it will pass. If it gets too much for you to cope with, your doctor may want to give you an anti-depressant for a short time. Many find this a help, but realize it is a temporary measure. Gradual reduction from these drugs is advisable.

Depression may manifest itself in ways other than extreme sadness. Here are some of them: sighing; sluggishness; headaches; nausea; constipation; heavy limbs; feeling bloated; needing more sleep; time passing slowly; losing interest in people; feeling that people do not want to see you; isolating yourself; losing interest in

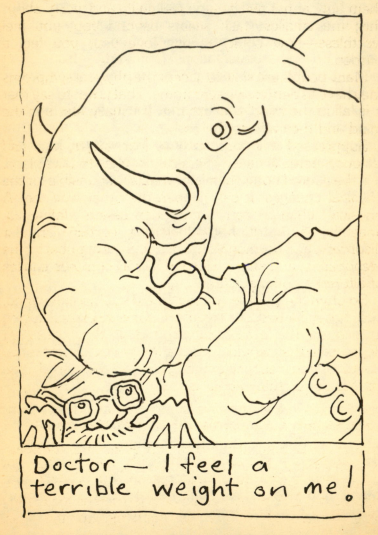

Doctor — I feel a terrible weight on me!

appearance; loss of appetite; compulsive eating (particularly sweet foods); being annoyed out of proportion to the situation; feeling a black cloud or shape over your head or on your shoulders; finding mornings are worse and having to force yourself from the oblivion of sleep; people you love seeming far away—you know you love them but cannot feel it—you feel guilty and worry about this; the smallest task seems beyond you; you feel worthless—how could anyone love you; you feel a burden.

Many people are slow to accept the physical symptoms they have as depressive symptoms. That is not to say that it is 'all in the mind'—far from it. It usually starts in the mind and then affects the body.

Suppressed emotions such as fear, anger, hurt and jealousy, actually cause chemical changes to take place. It is the altered body chemistry that is responsible for the physical changes. It can happen the other way too. A physical change can cause depression. Influenza, anaemia, bad nutrition, food allergies, certain glandular disorders, and hormonal changes such as at puberty, the menopause, and after childbirth, are all common causes of altered emotional states.

So often the sufferer will say 'If I did not feel exhausted, sick, heavy-limbed, etc. I would not be depressed.' In fact, it is often the other way around. If they were not depressed, they would not have the physical symptoms. So until you recognize that you are depressed, you cannot do anything about it.

Depression Caused By Sad Circumstances

It would be unnatural not to be depressed after the death of a loved one, a divorce, losing a job, or any other sad event. The sad person may be anxious, tearful, and withdrawn. This phase should be regarded as the resting time when the sufferer is adjusting to the loss.

Well-meaning friends often urge the sufferer not to cry. This is a great mistake. 'Permission' to grieve must be given. The pain or embarrassment of the onlookers should not be considered. If grief is repressed or pushed down ('isn't she brave, she is behaving so normally'), it may emerge later as physical or depressive illness.

Depression Caused By Buried Emotions

RIP

Lack of love
Resentment
Disappointment
Frustration
Rejection
Anger
Guilt
Fear.

Some people recover from chronic depression when a skilled therapist uncovers childhood trauma such as rejection, sexual abuse, or lack of love. For many it is only necessary to accept that their depression comes from 'listening to old scripts', and other people's views of themselves. You could think of your mind as a cellar. If the door is closed, it stays dark and damp, and old fears and resentments grow like mushrooms. If fresh air is allowed in, and the walls are white-washed, it could be a storehouse for the fruit from the orchard. The decision to open the cellar door may be hard. It may appear to be safer to stay depressed. The choice is with the sufferer.

Since you were a child, your feelings about yourself have been formed from the opinion of those around you. These messages from the past should be left behind. They can be completely wrong or may have been misinterpreted by you. The feelings of the child 'I must be a bad girl because mother/father has left me', need not grow to 'I must be worthless because my wife/husband has left me'.

As an adult you can let go of the past, 'old scripts', and other people's opinions of you, and start being kind to yourself.

Forgiving brings great healing. You can begin by forgiving yourself for being such an 'unworthy person'. Anger, hate, resentment, all dissolve when there is real forgiveness.

'I will never forgive him/her' really means that the child in your make-up is sulking.

Obsessive self-interest will soon make you a tiresome person, but compassionate self-awareness is essential if the quality of life is to be improved. Low self-esteem is a major factor in depressive illness.

Do you make any of the following mistakes?

Ways of Perpetuating Low Self-Esteem

1. Not accepting full responsibility for your own growth and well-being.
2. Lacking clear cut and meaningful goals to guide your decisions and reduce the time spent aimlessly drifting.
3. Not doing your own thinking and making your own decisions. Requiring the permission, confirmation, and agreement of others for what you think, say, and do.
4. Neglecting and ignoring your own needs in order to 'serve' others, not recognizing your own growth as your number one responsibility.
5. Being a 'professional people pleaser'.
6. Working at an occupation you heartily dislike, especially one that is not meaningful to you.
7. Setting yourself too high a standard to reach, and therefore constantly finding fault with yourself for not maintaining it.
8. Belittling yourself for mistakes and failures, indulging in destructive self-criticism.
9. Depending on others for a sense of importance rather than realizing that everyone is of equal worth and importance.
10. Not allowing yourself the right of full expression, not developing your own talents and capabilities.
11. Giving up before a job is finished and never getting the satisfaction of completion.
12. Comparing yourself with others as a gauge of your individual worth and importance. Believing you must prove your worth through superior performance.
13. Not speaking up for your own convictions, letting others ignore and belittle you. Not realizing that no one can insult or 'put you down' unless you accept his worth and authority over you.
14. Refusing to recognize your good characteristics, and

therefore building up a negative picture of yourself that is unrealistic.
15. Not recognizing your own needs for sleep, relaxation, satisfying work, companionship, good diet—not taking care of yourself.
16. Not letting others do things for you—or believing that they might want to.

Positive Acts to Raise Self-Esteem

1. Behave towards yourself as you would to a friend you love.
2. Beware of self-pity. Which old lady would you admire most? The one who says 'I can't be bothered to cook for one', or the one who takes care preparing her food and enjoys it.
3. Make time for yourself.
4. Think about what you really want—and write it down.
5. Little treats may help. Buy a pretty china cup and

Little treats help

saucer, silk scarf/tie, or house plant. *DO NOT* feel guilty about it. The guilt may arise not from spending money, but from being kind to a 'worthless person'.

6. Have your hair done.
7. Make a weekly appointment for a sauna or swim.

You are worth time and effort. Changing the way you think about yourself is the way out of depressive illness. How can others like you if you do not like yourself?

Depression Following Tension

How often have you heard people say that they were depressed when the examination finished, or after an unwelcome visitor had left. The depression does not arrive whilst the strain is still there, but comes when you have a chance to relax. Perhaps this is nature's way of forcing you to slow down. Physical exercise and a conscious effort to relax during stress could prevent this type of depression.

How Does A Depressed Person Look?

If he is very depressed, he could look round-shouldered, head bowed, slow moving with a shuffling walk, and mask-like expression, or he could be the joke-a-minute person who tries hard to cover up his inner misery by being the life and soul of the party.

What do Depressed People Say?

'My body is so heavy; life, relationships, work, have no meaning; I feel far away and isolated, even in a room full of people; I know I love my family but I cannot feel it; I have no interest in anything; I won't read the papers or watch the news in case there is anything that makes me sadder; the smallest physical task seems beyond me; washing and dressing is such an effort; everyone else looks so normal; I dread a visitor in case they can see how abnormal I feel; my relatives would be better off without me; I see everything through a grey mist'.

How Can I Heal Myself?

If your doctor has ruled out physical illness, he may want you to have a course of anti-depressant drugs. These help some people dramatically, but cannot erase bad memories, or the way you feel about yourself. Acknowledge that by positive thinking, you can stop the past, or the present, circumstances hurting you.

Creative Visualization

This means using your imagination in a positive way to cure symptoms of depression (or any illness). You may wonder how this simple measure could help, but try it and see—it takes time for the body to react to the positive images but it does work. By imagining scenes where you look well and confident, you are stimulating the chemicals necessary for your well-being. A woman in hospital who was immobilized after an accident, made a remarkable recovery when she started using this technique. In most of her waking hours she imagined she was playing tennis and her body responded to these positive images.

Using Your Body As A Weapon Against Depression

The Russians use hard physical work to cure depression—and it works. Although you may feel tired (unless you are withdrawing quickly) the worst thing you can do is lie in bed. Instead of pulling the blankets over your head in an attempt to shut out the world, force yourself to get up early and have breakfast. This helps to establish normal body rhythms and stops you turning day into night. Even if at first you can do no more than sit in front of breakfast television, at least you are making a start.

Normality must be reached for—it will not come without effort. Build up physical activity until you are really active. You may not enjoy it, but it has to be done. Accept that your head and muscles may ache. Force yourself to walk no matter how leaden your legs may feel. Exercise improves the circulation and stimulates the anti-anxiety and anti-depression hormones. If you are planning unaccustomed vigorous exercise, it is better to have your doctor's permission first.

Food and Depression

We are what we eat—during World War II people were physically healthier when sugar and fats were in short supply. It may be that sugar is an even worse offender than fat. The Eskimos who lived on large quantities of

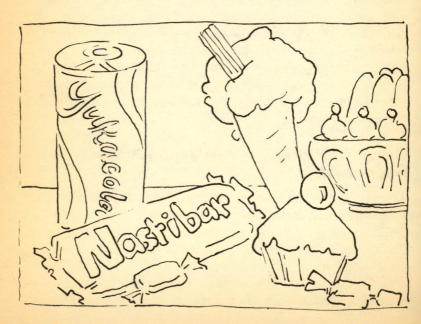

animal fat did not suffer coronary artery disease until they introduced sugar into their diet. American research suggests that more people die from cirrhosis of the liver through over-indulgence in sugar, than from high alcohol intake.

Cut down on or give up sugar, all sugar products, and anything made with white flour.

Food allergies can cause or deepen depression. A diet of boiled brown rice and spring water for a few days has helped many people discover what foods they are allergic to. They can introduce one food at a time until they find out what is upsetting them. This diet also gives the liver and kidneys a rest, and enables the body to get rid of toxins.

You can be fat and yet still be undernourished. A healthy diet is essential in depressive illness.

You may still feel very negative, and feel that your efforts are in vain, but others may have noticed encouraging little signs in you.

Things People Say When They Are 'Moving Forward'

'For the first time I could feel the effect my depression was having on my wife/children/secretary', etc.

'My facial muscles felt strange—then I realized that I was smiling at a baby'.

'I woke up thinking pleasurably about a cup of coffee instead of how I would get through the day.'

'I bought a packet of seeds. For the first time I was thinking beyond the gloomy moment.'

'I was halfway through a board meeting/the ironing/the weekly shopping, when I realized that I was not resenting every minute of it.'

'I actually started a conversation.'

'I forced myself to tidy the shed, then was astonished to find, when I went indoors, that two hours had passed'.

'I realized that the birds had not stopped singing. I had shut my ears to them.'

'For the first time in years my regular business trips to the States seemed like a normal thing to do.'

'I bought a book at the airport and did not feel thoroughly irritated when a child dropped ice cream on my shoe. They may seem small things, but I feel really free'.

Self-Help Groups For Depression

Working in a group towards health can be of great benefit. See if there is a depression self-help group in your area. Guard against an exchange of symptoms without a positive approach and be prepared to accept that someone close to you may feel threatened when they see you changing. They may feel safe when you are depressed and they are in the caring role. Reassure them that you are only changing your feelings about yourself, not them.

Suicidal Feelings

In withdrawal, suicidal feelings can come 'out of the blue'. Some people don't get them at all, others have vague feelings, some feel as if they are at risk. If you are worried, see your doctor as soon as possible. He may want you to take an anti-depressant for a while.

Many callers say, 'I have a wonderful family, why do I get overwhelming suicidal feelings?' Over-strained nerves often provoke suicidal thoughts, but in withdrawal, it may be an indication that you are cutting down too quickly.

The Samaritans are always there ready to listen. Many people say 'I had awful suicidal feelings, but felt I could not ring the Samaritans because I knew they were just feelings and that I would not do anything.' The Samaritans give up their time to comfort and support people. Use the service if you need it.

Agoraphobia

This is often thought of as fear of open spaces, but it is a great deal more wide-ranging. A man who can happily drive to work may be paralysed with fear if he has to travel by public transport. Even going to the local shop can be an impossible task for the agoraphobic.

Many people suffer agoraphobic symptoms both while on, and coming off tranquillizers. These will go eventually like all the other symptoms. Even people who were agoraphobic before they took pills, often recover because during withdrawal they face old fears and gradually overcome them. Don't push yourself whilst you are still physically low.

Dr Claire Weekes's book on agoraphobia is very helpful.

Creative visualization is helpful in agoraphobia too. Several times a day take a moment to relax, close your eyes, and see a television screen and make a picture of yourself looking happy and relaxed. Do it again and again until it is easy to imagine yourself with a smile on your face taking a short walk in the street. Keep at this until you extend your imaginary trips to crowded shops, or whatever you are most afraid of.

If any anxiety symptoms appear, practice abdominal breathing and put cold wet cloths on your face to control them. You will be surprised by what can happen when you give your brain the right messages.

In most people, the symptoms disappear when the physical symptoms improve, particularly if there was not a problem before taking tranquillizers.

Outbursts of Rage

This can happen as a side-effect and withdrawal reaction. When it happens whilst you are on tranquillizers it could be what is called the paradoxical effect. Instead of feeling calm and relaxed the user may feel disinhibited and full of rage. Mothers are often afraid they will hurt their children during these attacks. Losing your temper out of all proportion to the situation is distressing and very common. Help the people around you to understand this is temporary and not your real personality. Give them any literature you have about withdrawal, and take them to the support group where they will see other people with the same problem.

Your personality may have temporarily changed whilst you were on the pills. So often the cry is 'I just want to be the person I used to be.' Your old self is still there. It will come back. Some users have suppressed their emotions for so long that when the pills are taken away, they temporarily become aggressive and hard to live with. It is difficult for you and your family, but necessary for a while, to get you in touch with normal feelings again.

Hallucinations

If you are cutting down slowly, these should not trouble you. Some people prefer a more rapid withdrawal and are prepared to tolerate these symptoms when they understand why they are happening, and that they are not an indication that they are going mad. The looming faces so often seen are really an exaggeration of what normally happens just as we are about to drop off to sleep, although we are rarely aware of it, just as in alcohol withdrawal, spiders, reptiles, devils, etc. have been 'seen'. One woman 'saw' her father (who was three hundred miles away) so clearly that she made him a cup of coffee. She slowed down her withdrawal and had no further hallucinations. Hearing music, telephones ringing, and voices is often reported, but these too disappear as withdrawal is slowed down.

Perception Difficulties

Some of the action of the drugs is on the temporal lobe of the brain. During withdrawal, this area is trying to get back to normal. For a time this may result in temporal lobe symptoms. Perception difficulties are included. This means your senses (sight, sound, touch, taste and smell) may appear to be playing tricks on you. Your senses have been dulled by the drugs for so long that you have slowly become accustomed to altered perception. This may increase a little before it clears. Don't be alarmed if things seem odd at first. You will realize that this is how the world looked before drugs. Lights and colours may seem so bright at first that you need sunglasses. Many people have forgotten the pleasure of colour and are thrilled by their gardens. One woman kept scrubbing her carpet thinking it looked dull. When she came off her drugs she said she felt as though the colours were leaping out at her, they were so bright. Overbreathing also heightens

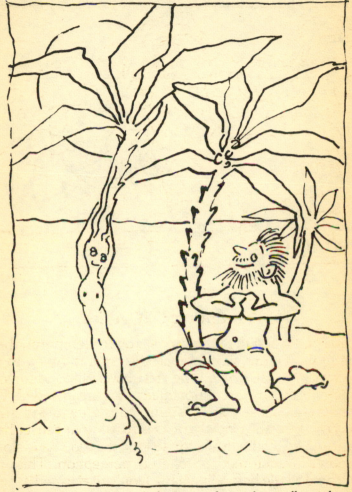

perception. If you see a dirty mark on the wall as a beetle, or a coat hanging behind the door as a person, these are perceptual disturbances. If there is no mark on the wall, nor a coat behind the door, and yet you see these things, these could be hallucinations. Many people say that faces seem to change as they look at them, or heads appear larger than they should be when they watch television. Buildings can appear too tall and thin, or bent at the top. These are temporary disturbances and will go in time.

Sound

The hypersensitivity to sound causes many family

arguments. The sufferer has to turn the sound on the television so low that no one else can hear it. Doorbells are often disconnected, and telephones covered with blankets or cushions. Sounds not normally noticed, like the click of a light switch, or a clock ticking, can be distressing to some.

Touch

Some people complain of pain when they are touched, or of discomfort when they touch a rough fabric. Others do not feel pain, but say everything feels odd—water feels like slime, objects that should feel rough feel smooth. For a time, one woman could not cook because everything felt like jelly. Even if the joint of meat was burnt black, it still felt like jelly when she put a knife in it.

Taste

Loss of taste or altered taste sensation is common. It may be a surprise to find chocolate tasting salty or something savoury tasting sweet, but it is only a temporary nuisance. Enormous numbers complain of a metallic taste in the mouth, others say it tastes bitter, sweet or creamy.

After several months of loss of taste, one woman was delighted when she could taste sprouts. Gradually the number of foods she could taste increased (so did her weight). Beware of overeating if this happens to you.

Smell

Some users report loss of smell, but others say even pleasant smells like perfume become unpleasant. One man had a smell like petrol in his nose for several weeks.

Shaking

Visible shaking, or feeling of shaking inside are common

symptoms. When we are nervous it is natural to shake. It will go, like all the other symptoms as your nervous system recovers. The shaking inside may be due to low blood sugar or caffeine from too much coffee or tea, or excessive cigarettes.

Eye Problems

Sore eyes and visual disturbances are common. Users often change their spectacles several times during withdrawal. Check with your oculist to make sure, but you will probably find that the blurred vision and sore eyes will clear up as withdrawal progresses. Pads of cotton wool soaked with witch-hazel on closed eyes may be soothing. Tinted lenses are helpful if you are sensitive to light.

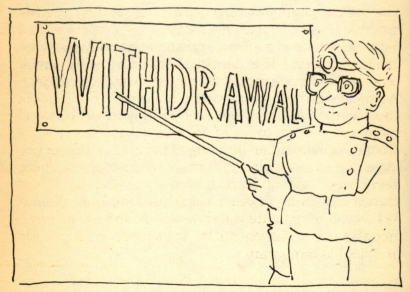

Chest Symptoms and Palpitations

Always see your doctor if you have chest pain. Many

have experienced tightness, numbness or pain in the chest or down the left arm. This could be another rebound effect. After you have been reassured by your doctor, accept the temporary discomfort, it will pass. Abdominal breathing often helps.

It is not surprising that people become convinced that there is something wrong with their hearts when they experience palpitations or missed beats. If you were running for a bus and your heart rate increased, it would not worry you. Because you are cutting down on drugs that have slowed the heart rate, you can expect a similar effect.

Abdominal Symptoms

The collicky pains and diarrhoea are usually diagnosed as 'Irritable Bowel Syndrome'. Many people have had barium meals and enemas, and some even have investigative surgery. The investigations invariably prove negative, and the symptoms disappear without treatment. A simple diarrhoea mixture may be helpful. The modern approach of a high fibre diet to the irritable bowel syndrome seems to increase symptoms during withdrawal. Diarrhoea can be a side-effect of tranquillizer use too and may start when the drugs are first taken. There have been several reports of people who have had chronic diarrhoea for years which has completely cleared 3–4 weeks after acute withdrawal in hospital. The slight incontinence experienced by some (particularly early morning) is temporary.

Urinary Symptoms

Frequency, burning, and incontinence are reported. Again, investigations usually prove negative. Treatment for infection is ineffective. If your doctor confirms there is no infection, drink plenty of water and be patient. Young and old, men and women, sometimes have slight (and temporary) urinary incontinence during withdrawal.

Influenza-like Symptoms

If you experience headaches, sore throat, stuffy nose, burning skin, it may be that you are cutting down too quickly. Some people recognize that they have had these symptoms for years. The influenza they experienced several times a year was when they ran out of pills, or forgot to take them on holiday. Many people remember a flu-like illness when their pills were stopped on admission to hospital for routine surgery. The symptoms always disappeared when they resumed taking their pills.

Hormone Imbalance

Most of the hormonal symptoms are at their worst when

the user is taking the full dose of tranquillizers. They may change during withdrawal, but return to normal when withdrawal is completed. For instance, all interest in sex may be lost whilst taking tranquillizers. The reverse may happen for a time during withdrawal before normality returns.

Some women who suffered heavy periods for years when they were on the pills, find they have a normal flow after withdrawal. Vaginal discharge, burning vulva, and increased pre-menstrual tension can also cause temporary discomfort.

Research has shown that a hormone called prolactin is increased whilst tranquillizers are taken. This stimulates lactation, and reports of breast symptoms are common. They range from a slight pale brown discharge to considerable quantities of milk. This has happened up to sixteen years after the last pregnancy. After you have been examined by your doctor, be patient and the symptoms will disappear when you are through withdrawal.

Men too report swollen tender breasts and slight discharge. They also complain of impotence, loss of seminal fluid, and pain in the testicles. Some have eruptions of adolescent acne.

When the hormone levels return to normal all the symptoms disappear.

Jaw Pain

This can be severe, and is described as a pain boring up through the jaw, usually on one side at a time. It seems at its worst when the neck muscles are tense; when lying down; or when taking hot food or drink.

The pain resembles toothache, and unfortunately many people have had a full dental extraction in an attempt to gain relief. The pain persists after dental treatment, and even people who have had dentures for years have experienced this 'toothache'. The jaw pain (and all pain associated with withdrawal) goes, but if it is too much to bear, see your doctor. Many people have had dramatic relief from a drug called Tegretol. It is the drug used for the notoriously painful condition trigeminal neuralgia. Withdrawal jaw pain closely resembles this. Aspirin or Paracetemol rarely help this pain. Some people have been helped by having their neck and shoulders massaged, or by sucking ice, or rinsing their mouths with whisky. Others have been helped by having a removable plastic shield, called an occlusion splint, fitted over their bottom teeth. They wear this at night and it prevents jaw clenching. Ask your dentist for advice.

Trigeminal neuralgia can be a symptom of depression. Perhaps that is where the old term 'face ache' for a miserable person comes from.

Stinging or aching in the front teeth is also reported. Check that you are eating properly. Low blood sugar can trigger off this jaw pain.

Muscle Pains and Swollen Painful Joints

Aching muscles, cramps, and joint pains are very common. The drugs have artificially relaxed them for so long that they have forgotten how to work efficiently. The stiff, sore heavy limbs will recover. Some people say they feel as though someone is pulling them back when they are walking. Massage, yoga, swimming and warm baths are all helpful. Accept that your muscles need to be re-educated and work hard by slowly building up movement.

The muscles of the neck and shoulders are particularly troublesome. You may find yourself walking around with your shoulders almost touching your ears. Ask your family to gently press your shoulders down when they see you doing this, or pretend that you have a heavy weight in each hand. Sitting on a hard chair, pushing down on your hands and slightly raising your buttocks may help to exercise neck muscles. Sitting up in a chair with a covered hot water bottle between the shoulders can be helpful.

Some doctors prescribe quinine for the muscle spasm.

Perhaps the joint pains can be explained by the strain resulting from abnormal muscle action.

Feelings of the Ground Moving

Many people say that they feel as if the ground is moving when they walk, or that they are walking on cotton wool. It can be alarming but does settle down as withdrawal progresses. This unsteady gait (ataxia) can be experienced in severe anxiety states where no drugs are being used.

Tingling, Numbness, Burning Sensations

Many people complain of tingling and numbness in hands and feet (although the feelings can be anywhere), and also feelings like electric shocks going through the body. Some of the tingling may be due to overbreathing. It could be that an exaggeration of normal nerve impulses is the reason for the electric shock feelings. All these feelings and the burning in the spine, vulva and inner thighs (or elsewhere) also disappear when withdrawal is complete.

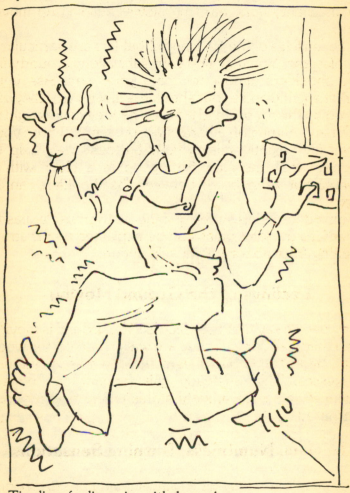

Tingling feelings in withdrawal

Changes in Body Temperature

Some people complain they are 'on fire'. Others say they

feel icy cold, or cold one minute and hot the next. Feeling hot, with or without profuse sweating is often a feature of drug withdrawal. If you are very cold perhaps moving more or massaging the affected parts would improve circulation.

Sore Mouth

There are frequent reports of painful/cracked/glossy/ swollen tongues; mouth ulcers; gum boils; cracks at the corners of the mouth and sore lips. These symptoms may be a reflection of the nutritional state of the body, particularly in the long-term user. Even if the diet seems adequate there is often so much disturbance in the digestive system that absorption of essential minerals and vitamins could be impaired.

Falling Hair

Users are often delighted to see new hair growing again as they recover.

Skin Problems

These should always be investigated in case there is another cause. The ones most commonly reported are: dryness, itching, a dry scaly rash (often on the hands or over the bridge of the nose and on to the cheeks), spontaneous bruising and skin breaking easily. Minor cuts often take a long time to heal. Many people notice a change in skin colour. It can have a slightly jaundiced or pale brown appearance. Often a dramatic improvement can be seen in the condition of the skin even in the early days of withdrawal.

Dental Problems

The high incidence of premature tooth loss (apart from extractions because of the jaw pain) in people who have been on tranquillizers for years is another pointer to inadequate nutrition. (The same may be said for split nails.)

Vitamin and Mineral Deficiency

During illness or stress the body's need for vitamins and minerals is increased. Common deficiencies are: iron, calcium, magnesium, vitamin C (particularly if you smoke) and vitamin B complex. It is advisable to have advice about which supplements you need and the length of time you should take them. For instance, many people take vitamin B6 for pre-menstrual tension not realizing that if they take one of the B vitamins in isolation they deplete their store of the other B vitamins.

4.

WORKING TOGETHER

Withdrawal Support Groups

Accepting and sharing problems with other people has always been good therapy. It is essential to be in a relaxed setting where you can grieve, have a panic attack, or make frequent trips to the lavatory without embarrassment. By expressing exactly what you feel, you give others permission to do the same.

There are often amusing moments even in the most unhappy situations. Sharing these is good medicine. One group member turned the meeting into a pantomime when she described the panic attack she experienced whilst working as a sales demonstrator in a supermarket.

Another young woman announced that she had come to terms with the temporary incontinence, 'All you need is to wear boots—you can slowly fill them up and nobody knows!'

Guard against endless discussions on how inappropriate or harmful your drug treatment has been. It is in the past. Air your views on the subject, then leave it behind.

If you are lucky enough to get through withdrawal without any drugs for symptomatic relief, be grateful, and do not scold those who cannot. They may be disappointed that they need anti-depressants or other drugs for a time. The aim is for everyone to be drug-free, but some people may need temporary medication to achieve this.

Remember too that you cannot know the medical history of others in the group and there may be a very good reason why they are on certain drugs.

Relaxation

This is not just a set of silly exercises to fill in the afternoon. Muscles that are shouting for a chemical that you have stopped taking have to be re-trained.

If you tie a tight band around your arm, what happens to your hand? You will certainly get pain, swelling, loss of movement and an altogether unhealthy hand. You are effectively doing the same to your head by tension in the neck and shoulder muscles. Decreased circulation to the head causes headaches, sinus pains, jaw pain, ear problems (including tinnitus) depression, confusion and more. Is it worth working on your neck and shoulders?

What You Can Do

Start by asking the members of the group who only want to chatter to leave the room.

Sit in a circle on stools or hard chairs. Notice how many members are pulling one or both shoulders up to their ears, and how many heads are pulled to one side or pulled down and back with chins poking forward. The reason for this is that in withdrawal, muscles on the side of the neck shorten. This unbalances the head, and because it is so heavy (about one and a half stones), it puts a strain on the neck and shoulders that goes right down the spine through the pelvis to the knees. That is why so many people complain of weak aching knees. Notice how many people are pulling their feet back under the chair, or have their legs crossed.

Retraining muscles involves learning where tensions are and, without causing more tension by trying too hard, letting them go. The blur of aches and pains all over that people endure are often nothing more than tension. The pain-relieving chemicals produced by the brain are disturbed during withdrawal and that is why pain from old injuries or scars often reappears for a time.

If there is a teacher of the Alexander technique in your area you would not regret money spent on some lessons. The principle of the teaching is to show you how to live in the world without your body reacting to stress.

How to Sit

If you lower your gaze your head will assume a better position. Sit with the spine straight but not rigid. Imagine

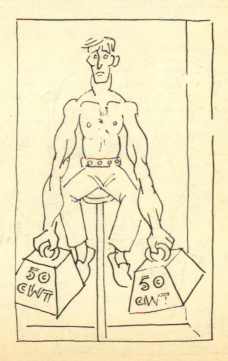

you have heavy weights in your hands, and let them droop towards the floor. This will bring your shoulders down. Now place your hands, palms upwards, on your lap.

Shake each leg in turn then place feet (without shoes) on the floor. Imagine you are wearing heavy boots.

It is a good plan to start all group meetings in this position, even if you are in easy chairs. It may take some persuasion. People often feel vulnerable in this position and 'protect' themselves by tightening the shoulders, crossing the arms over the chest and crossing the legs, the moment they say anything involving feelings, e.g. 'My wife does not understand panic attacks', or 'I saw my psychiatrist yesterday'.

Try to be aware of how you are holding yourself whatever you are doing. It is possible to iron without

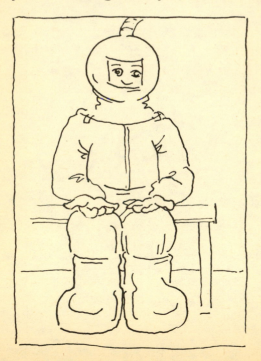

fiercely gripping the iron, to drive without grappling with the steering wheel. Dishes still get washed if you don't press your knees back and tense your neck.

Even confrontation is possible without tightening up. You will feel much more in control facing an angry boss if you are aware of your muscles and breathing. An afternoon spent entertaining a tiresome relative will affect you much less if you make a conscious effort to relax.

'What am I doing with my shoulders?'

Exercises Sitting in a Chair

1. Check the position of your head and neck and breathe in through the nose as you loosely lift the shoulders, breathe out noisily as you drop them, and go limp in the chair. Try it eight times,.
2. Roll each shoulder first back then forward in a circle

Keep calm when facing an angry boss

(keep the arm limp). After you have circled both shoulders eight times in each direction, try doing both together.

3. Raise arms to the ceiling and stretch without straining, then let them fall loosely towards the floor.

4. Add any shoulder or arm exercises you know and stand up to do a few loose swinging arm movements.

5. To exercise the legs draw eight circles with each big toe, clockwise and anticlockwise.

6. Finish by standing up and loosely shaking the whole body.

Shaking increases circulation and lets fear out. Dogs don't stop themselves shaking when they are afraid. Don't try to control nervous shaking. Stand up and encourage it. If it is not suppressed the need to shake (and to cry or be angry) will diminish.

Don't push yourself to do more exercise than you can manage, but carry on slowly even if it hurts. It may be

uncomfortable. Remember the tight arm band previously mentioned? Taking it off the arm would make the hand feel more uncomfortable for a time, but it would be curative. In the same way, some people have held their head and shoulders tight for so long that they need the help of an osteopath to free the joints.

In tranquillizer withdrawal it is not advisable to tighten

groups of muscles before letting them relax. Because the muscles are not behaving normally it increases spasms. It is better to use your imagination. Pretend that your feet/legs/trunk/arms etc. are being bathed in warm water or sunlight. This allows them to go slack and heavy. Avoid using the word relax. Some people are so frustrated by their unsuccessful attempts at relaxation that the word is a trigger for more tension.

Massage

Work in pairs. Allow your partner to sit in the chair in the position that has been discussed, with closed eyes. Support their forehead and gently massage the scalp from the hair line to the back of the neck. If headaches are a problem, support their head on your chest and work with both hands, stroking their brow with the first fingers from the centre to the temples, using firm strokes.

You and your partner will soon get over the embarrassment of being touched when you realize how relaxing massage can be. Continue to support the forehead and with the other hand move the muscles of the neck on both sides of the spine in a circular movement. Switch off your intellect and let your hands do the work. Next place your hands over the shoulders with the fingers pointing towards the chest and the thumbs on the back. Use these to massage the muscles of the shoulders. Find out from your partner any areas that need particular attention. Continue by supporting your partner with your arm across the top of their chest, tipping them forward and working around both shoulder blades and down each side of the spine. Finish off by stroking lightly and rapidly from the head down the back. Place one hand on the upper and one on the underside of the arm and use the same stroking to the finger tips. Repeat with the other arm. Take at least fifteen minutes over the massage. The person in the chair might want to sit for few minutes, enjoying feeling more relaxed, before doing the same for you.

Visualization

Continue the relaxation session by taking time to get as comfortable as possible on the floor using blankets, cushions or coats. You may not feel cold when you lie down but as you relax your temperature could go down. (People who feel unhappy on the floor can be supported in a chair.) Lie down, shoulders relaxed, palms up. If you have back pain you may be more comfortable with your knees slightly bent and your feet on the floor.

Start with five minutes abdominal breathing, and try to be aware of your breathing during the session. Arrange for someone to play a relaxation tape. Choose one that has a passage of soothing music at the end. Close your eyes and imagine you are with the group or with someone who has made you feel secure in the past. Let the tape 'wash over you' without struggling to concentrate.

During the music section at the end think about the questions below.

Choices

If there is no organic reason for your emotional illness, or if you are over the early months of withdrawal, you can choose to be well. This involves looking after your whole being not just your body and it may be necessary to change the way you think. First ask yourself if there are any rewards in staying ill:

Does being ill bring more care and attention from others or protect you from issues you are unwilling to face? Are you avoiding rejection/going out into the world/being an adult/admitting you are with the wrong partner? Because of the illness are you able to avoid responsibility/ risks/social interaction/a sexual relationship/failure or physical effort?

If you are not doing any of these, are you hanging on to sadness or hurtful feelings from the past in order to justify the way you are?

Letting Go of the Past

In the quiet time during relaxation imagine you are holding on to the string of a large balloon. There is a basket on the bottom of the balloon. Without straining to remember everything, put into the basket anything that has ever hurt you since before your birth: lack of love, rejection, failure, hurtful things people have said and done, grief, pain, frustration, anger, feelings of worthlessness, guilt, shame, or anything else lurking around. Now raise your hand briefly in a conscious attempt to let go of the string, and watch the balloon float out of sight. It may take several weeks to get some particularly hurtful things into the basket, but when you have managed it you will feel the release.

Sharing the 'basket' experience at the end of the session is helpful in two ways. Fellow feeling in the group is cemented by the realization that we all have similar hurts and insecurities, and also the person who is unwilling to relinquish the past hurts can use the group as a 'sounding board' to reflect his or her own thoughts in order to discover why there should be reluctance to let go. Often there is laughter during this sharing time. One man amused a group by saying, 'It was a struggle, but I got my mother-in-law in the basket this week.'

If you are a private person and do not want to share your feelings it is still a useful exercise.

Be patient with yourself if you suffered a bereavement or other sad experience whilst you were on tranquillizers. You may have to work through those feelings again as you withdraw, even if you feel rationally that the experience is in the past.

Is There a Danger of Becoming Too Dependent on the Helper?

Most ill people need to be dependent for a time. As they recover, they gain confidence and self-esteem, and reliance on the helper disappears. The odd time that this is not the case, it is up to the helper to encourage independence by gradually withdrawing attention unless really positive moves are made by the user.

Caution for Helpers

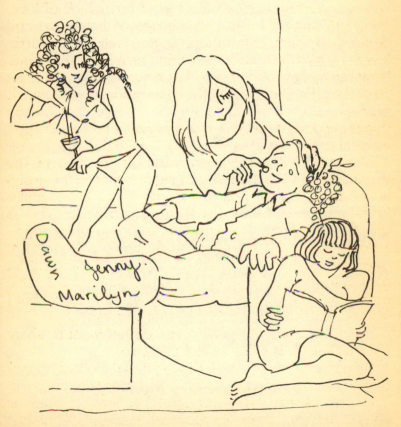

No matter how sincere you are in your efforts to help,

there will always be someone who will direct their anger at you. Try not to be hurt by this, however unjustified you feel it to be. You may be serving a useful purpose. The person may feel it safer to express anger outside the family circle. It will be upsetting, particularly if you are not feeling completely recovered yourself. Get used to it—it will happen again.

It is good to have positive talk times, when all talk of withdrawal symptoms is banned, or to have social outings away from where the group usually meets. Marvellous things happen when people get together to work towards being well. It is touching to see how much strangers can care about each other if they are given the opportunity. If someone weeps, don't be in a hurry to make tea—that may only be to save your own embarrassment. A box of tissues in one hand and the other on the shoulder of the distressed person usually means more.

Even if you do get a bit discouraged at times, the work in groups is very rewarding. It is exciting to see people looking healthier as they cut down their drugs, and to see confidence and animation return.

Note for Relatives

People in withdrawal need a great deal of care and understanding. It is a help to be relieved of as much responsibility as possible, particularly in the early days. Read all the literature you can find on the subject and attend group meetings with your partner if possible. Take care of yourself too, it can be exhausting looking after someone in withdrawal.

Complementary Medicine

Many people have found comfort and relief from withdrawal symptoms or symptoms that pre-dated taking drugs when they have consulted practitioners of alternative medicine (see page 108 for Useful Addresses). Seek out a registered practitioner and do not expect miracles after one or two visits. It is essential to follow a course of treatment. Some of these treatments are available on the National Health. Many people are reluctant to spend money on their health, yet willing to

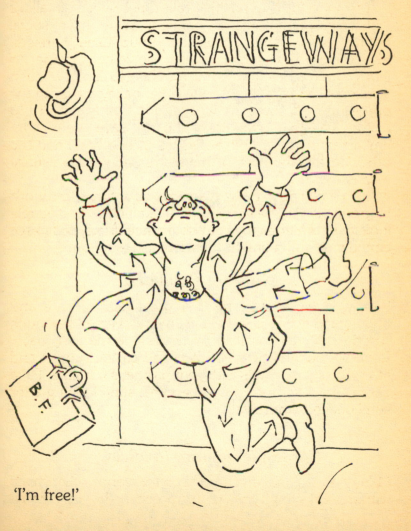

'I'm free!'

give up a great deal of their weekly wage for cigarettes or alcohol.

Holistic Healing

Often great emphasis is placed on the physical, emotional, and mental health of the individual. Spiritual well-being is ignored. 'How can that possibly affect the way I am feeling?' Some believe that this is the most important area to explore.

Many have discovered or renewed their faith in God by the experience of nervous illness.

In the search for inner peace and relief from 'dis-ease', some people have found spiritual healing the answer. Following the discipline of yoga or meditation has been the way for others.

Suffering Is Not All Bad

It can be a time for learning, and because of new insight, a time for reaching out to those in distress around you.

5.

KEEP GOING—YOU *WILL* MAKE IT

Points to Remember

1. Hold your head up—you are brave. What has happened is *not* your fault.
2. Do your 'homework'—breathing exercises, diet, exercise, relaxation, cultivating optimistic thoughts.
3. Remember it has taken you a long time to get into this state. Recovery won't come overnight.
4. You are the only person who knows what it feels like to be in your body. Ignore the person who says you should be well after two weeks.
5. *Smile*—the real you is still there!

Case Histories

Here are some stories about people who have come through withdrawal. You should find them encouraging.

Marion was prescribed Valium when her husband died thirteen years earlier. Over the years she was so occupied raising four children that she just kept swallowing the pills. She became so tired, it was an effort to get out of bed and she wondered if it had anything to do with the Valium. Her doctor sent her to a consultant who was helpful and understanding. It was suggested that she came off her Valium quickly in hospital. She was given other drugs to help her symptoms, and was Valium-free two weeks later. She stayed in hospital for a further three weeks. Her physical appearance changed quickly, and by the time she left hospital, her skin and eyes had come back to life.

For a few days in hospital, she had felt overwhelmed by grief for her husband. The pills had suppressed her emotions for so long she was relieved to be able to cry.

She has coped well since she got home, although at first she was depressed. Six months later, she looks very well and is patiently waiting for her sleeping pattern to return to normal. The spaces between the 'down' spells are getting longer and longer. Her friends are delighted to see her sense of humour returning to normal.

Maurice, aged thirty-seven, found it difficult to establish a normal sleeping pattern after frequent business trips to America. Mogadon was prescribed and he found the jet-lag easier to cope with. After three months he was not travelling so much and felt he did not need the tablets. His insomnia became worse than he had ever known it. He had palpitations and a tight feeling in his chest, and also had digestive problems.

His doctor was kind and sympathetic but said he did not think Maurice had been on the tablets long enough for dependence to have developed. The doctor suggested going back on the full dose to see what happened.

Maurice's symptoms were much improved when he visited the surgery a week later. His doctor said that he had discussed the case with his partner who had two patients who had experienced similar problems, although they had taken the tablets over a longer period.

Complete withdrawal took six weeks. For the following three weeks Maurice felt 'off colour' but did not have any dramatic symptoms. After that he was back to normal.

Ann is twenty-seven years old and was prescribed

Ativan (3 mg) when she was told her baby was mentally handicapped. She coped well, but felt very down. After about four months, she felt increasingly anxious. Her doctor suggested she doubled the dose of Ativan. The anxiety lessened, but she had frequent headaches and lost her balance very easily. She thought she was run down due to increasingly heavy periods. Her husband complained that she was not the same person, and suggested a holiday.

Ann thought she might have more energy if she reduced her pills to half the dose. Two days later she felt very ill. She had diarrhoea, vomiting, nasal congestion, and a sore throat. The doctor diagnosed a virus. Ann had not slept so she resumed her full dose of Ativan. The symptoms dramatically disappeared. She recognized the same symptoms nine months later when she forgot to pack her pills when she stayed with an aunt. She thought it could have something to do with the pills, but her doctor assured her they were safe and non-addictive.

The heavy bleeding persisted and she was admitted to hospital for investigations. The ward sister kept the pills. Her skin burned, she felt sick, and the world looked strange again. She was sure it was the pills this time. Her doctor was kind, but said that this was unlikely.

A phone call to a friend, a Community Psychiatric Nurse, gave her some hope. He advised her to cut down slowly. Three months through withdrawal she noticed her periods were not so heavy and the sinus pains that had plagued her for the two years on Ativan had gone. There were times during withdrawal when she felt unwell, but she felt her old self returning. Her husband remarked how different she looked. It is now nine months since she completed withdrawal. Getting off to sleep, and palpitations, are still a problem, but apart from these, she feels well and is delighted to be drug-free. She is also delighted that the hair she lost during withdrawal has grown in again.

Andrew, aged twenty-nine, was prescribed Ativan eight years before for examination nerves. He was not sure why he carried on taking them. He had increased the dose twice during those eight years, but had not changed it during the past two years. He was then on 6 mg per day.

He complained to a friend (a dentist) that he had burning spinal pain, numbness, pins and needles in his limbs, and blurred vision. The friend said that it sounded like multiple sclerosis, and urged him to seek medical help. His doctor sent him to a neurologist who said he could find nothing wrong.

The doctor and neurologist suggested a holiday. During Andrew's second miserable week, he saw a report in a local paper about a support group for people having trouble with tranquillizers. It was explained to him by the group that his body had become accustomed to the drugs, and that he was having withdrawal symptoms, even though he was still taking the tablets.

Three months after complete withdrawal, the spinal pain and other symptoms had disappeared. He made a weekly telephone call to the support group for reassurance when he felt down, or had the occasional panic attack. He cut down on coffee and cigarettes, and ate a balanced diet with vitamin and mineral supplements. He feels that swimming helped him to recover, although he admits it was a tremendous effort at first to go to the local pool twice a week. He is now very well, and supporting (by telephone) several people in his area who are withdrawing.

Nigel, aged forty-nine, started taking Librium twelve years ago when professional worries were making him anxious. Two years ago before surgery for a hernia, he decided to stop taking the pills. The surgery was straightforward, but his recovery was very slow. By the time he left hospital, he was suffering from severe insomnia, palpitations, anxiety worse than he had ever experienced before, and a feeling of tightness in his chest. He was puzzled by how ill he felt, but thought it was weakness after the operation.

During the same year, he complained of nausea and severe abdominal pain. Hospital tests proved negative. He had his spectacles changed three times, trying to correct visual disturbances. So many things were going wrong, he thought his wife must have been right when she said, 'It is all in your mind,' although the severe pain he then developed in his right shoulder and in his neck, seemed real enough to him.

Now, eighteen months later, he feels better, but still has some symptoms. Insomnia, palpitations, headaches, and irritability are still a problem, but very much less than they were. He was never tempted at any time during those eighteen months to go back on the pills. He tried alcohol in the evenings, but it did not seem to help.

The experience has changed his attitude to life. He now makes time to relax each day during lunch. What used to be a hurried sandwich and numerous cups of coffee, is now a salad with meat or cheese and fruit, and fifteen minutes lying on the office floor listening to a relaxation tape and being aware of his breathing. He is amazed by how different he feels at the end of the day.

Grace, aged sixty-seven, was prescribed Tranxene six years ago because she was 'run down' after nursing her husband through a long illness. She had always been a strong outward-looking woman who spent a lot of her time helping the young mothers and the elderly in her area. She saw her doctor because she was becoming increasingly confused and agoraphobic. She was given a tonic and told to rest.

Her daughter telephoned her saying that she had read an article in a woman's magazine saying the elderly should have greatly reduced doses of tranquillizers because they cannot excrete them at the same rate as the young. Because of this, the elderly are often confused and have frequent falls. Weight is also an important factor. So often a person weighing $7\frac{1}{2}$ stones is prescribed the same dose as a heavyweight of 15 stones.

Grace telephoned the Citizens' Advice Bureau to see if there was any help in her area. After a telephone call to the support group (and to her doctor for his permission), she started slow withdrawal. She had been cutting down for six weeks when she felt her old self returning. Her family said she had lost the dead look from her eyes and her skin looked a healthier colour.

She rang the group regularly for explanation of a symptom or for reassurance. Her main problems were headaches, slight incontinence, and a feeling that her bottom was 'not there'. The agoraphobia was much better by the time her drugs were reduced to half, although by this time she was a bit shaky outside because she felt the ground was moving when she walked.

Her positive attitude to any problem was a great help to her. She was more confident when she pushed a shopping trolley. Walking with a stick was the next step. She now walks unaided, supports others (often using humour to ease tension), and is excited about her holiday when she is taking her grandson camping.

Robin, aged twenty-three, was given Valium as a muscle relaxant when he injured his knee playing rugby. After four months he was walking normally and decided to stop taking the Valium. He became anxious and depressed and could not sleep. This was very unusual for him. He thought the injury must have upset him more than he realized. The same thing happened again when he stopped the Valium three weeks later.

His doctor said he had become physically dependent, and apologized for not watching him more closely. With regular support from his doctor, and a slow withdrawal programme, Robin did very well. He learnt to meditate and felt that this helped him to accept the insomnia and physical discomfort.

Laura's story illustrates how a combination of a psychiatrist who only knows half the story, plus repeated dosing with tranquillizers and anti-depressants can result in what appears to be a serious psychiatric problem.

Laura began to suffer from depression when she suspected that her husband was being unfaithful to her. He said she was imagining things and should see a doctor. Her GP agreed she was depressed and sent her to a psychiatrist who, after talking to (and believing) her husband, told her that her problems were due to an unhappy childhood, and that she needed psychotherapy. Laura accepted this, although her doubts about her husband persisted.

Two years later, her sister-in-law told the psychiatrist that Laura's suspicions about her husband were correct. But by then Laura had been prescribed a range of anti-depressants and tranquillizers, had had electroconvulsive therapy (ECT), and had become convinced that she was a mentally sick person. Her psychiatrist's diagnosis was to haunt her for many years. A painful divorce followed and due to the periods which Laura had spent as an in-patient, care and custody of her children was given to her ex-husband.

The next ten years Laura describes as 'living in a void'. Although she tried to build a new life for herself, and discharged herself from the psychiatrists' care, she was prescribed the same drugs by her GP. Because of her efforts to give them up, and not understanding her physical dependence on them, she went in and out of withdrawal as her medication was changed or suspended.

Although before her marriage she had never suffered from anxiety, she now complained of phobias, insomnia, stomach discomforts, eye problems and skin rashes. She had little contact with her children and often wondered if her psychiatrist had been right about her. Her medical record read like a disaster, describing her as 'neurotic', unable to cope with life, and 'possibly schizophrenic'. Eventually her prescriptions for Valium and Mogadon were handed to her by her doctor's receptionist with no review or consultation.

Two years ago, her sister-in-law intervened again and persuaded her that her pills could be the main cause of her present condition and took her to a tranquillizer withdrawal group. She checked with her GP and he said there was no reason why she should continue with the drugs if she did not want to.

Laura was impatient to finish her drugs, and came off them more rapidly than she was advised. Her withdrawal was 'a nightmare', but she was also very excited by it because she was experiencing emotions that she had not felt for years. Symptoms that she had experienced over the years worsened, and new ones appeared, but with group support she continued. She became aggressive and hostile. Her restlessness and alternating agoraphobia and claustrophobia increased until she was staying first with one friend and then another, packing her bags every few days to move on again.

Fear of riding in cars (her lack of co-ordination and judgement had relegated her to the passenger seat), nightmares, hallucinations, constant throbbing headaches, heightened perception, and all the time the nagging fear that she was either mad, or the victim of a serious physical illness, made life hell.

As the symptoms eased and the depression lifted, Laura saw that her problems started with her first misdiagnosis. She learned to 'let go' of the sadness of the past and have hope about the future. It is a great joy to her that she sees more of her children who now see her as a 'real' person, and are impressed that she has a full-time job.

Her image of herself as a sick person has gone.

During the years that Laura was dependent on the benzodiazepines she had investigations for suspected ulcer, heart disease, skin rashes, dry eye problems, and arthritis. *None* of the tests proved positive and since she has come through withdrawal *all* the symptoms have gone.

She now looks forward to being a grandmother, has found that her old interest in photography is still there, and has joined her local historical society.

APPENDIX

List of Benzodiazepines available before limited prescribing

Brand Name	Generic Name	Length of Action	Strength	Description
Alupram	Diazepam	Long	2 mg	white, scored tablet marked Steinhard, with D over tablet strength on reverse.
			5 mg	as above, yellow.
			10 mg	as above, blue
Atensine	Diazepam	Long	2 mg	white, scored tablet marked BERK with tablet strength on one side.
			5 mg	as above, yellow.
			10 mg	as above, blue.
Evacalm	Diazepam	Long	2 mg	white, scored tablet.
			5 mg	yellow scored tablet.
Solis	Diazepam	Long	2 mg	violet/turquoise capsule marked SOLIS with strength.
			5 mg	violet/mauve capsule.
Valium	Diazepam	Long	2 mg	white, scored tablet marked ROCHE 2
			5 mg	yellow scored tablet tablet marked ROCHE 5

Brand Name	Generic Name	Length of Action	Strength	Description
			10 mg	blue scored tablet marked ROCHE 10
		Long	2.5 mg	Off-white cherry flavoured suspension.
			5 ml	
Surem	Nitrazepam	Long	5 mg	mauve/grey capsule marked SUREM 5.
Unicomnia	Nitrazepam	Long	5 mg	white scored tablet.
Dalmane	Flurazepam	Long	15 mg	grey/yellow capsule.
			30 mg	grey/black capsule.
Euhypnos	Temazepam	Medium	10 mg	green gelatin capsule marked 10.
Euhypnos forte	Temazepam	Medium	20 mg	green gelatin capsule.
Normison	Temazepam	Medium	10 mg	yellow capsule marked WYETH.
			20 mg	yellow capsule marked WYETH 20
Halcion	Triazolam	Very short	125 mcg	purple oval scored tablet tablet marked Upjohn 10.
			500 mcg	blue oval scored tablet marked Upjohn 17.
Tranxene	Clorazepate	Long	7.5 mg	maroon/grey capsule marked 7.5 mg with symbol
			15 mg	Pink/grey capsule marked 7.15 mg with symbol.
Frisium	Clobazam	Long	10 mg	blue capsule marked FRISIUM.

Brand Name	Generic Name	Length of Action	Strength	Description
Serenid-D	Oxazepam	Short	10 mg	white tablet marked WYETH and 10 on reverse.
Serenid			15 mg	as above with 15 on reverse
Serenid Forte			30 mg	red/green capsule marked WYETH
Valrelease	Diazepam	Long	10 mg	blue/light blue capsule marked ROCHE in red.
Librium	Chlordia-zepoxide	Long	5 mg 10 mg 25 mg	green/yellow tablets marked LIBRIUM or ROCHE
			5 mg	yellow/green capsule marked ROCHE 5 or LIBRIUM.
			10 mg	black/green capsule marked ROCHE 10 or LIBRIUM.
Almazine	Lorazepam	Medium	1 mg	green oval scored tablet marked MAS on one side, L over strength on reverse.
Ativan	Lorazepam	Medium	1 mg	blue oblong scored tablet marked WYETH.
			2.5 mg	as above, yellow.
Mogadon	Nitrazepam	Long	5 mg	white scored tablets with two semi-circles.
			5 mg	purple/black capsule marked ROCHE 5.
Nitrados	Nitrazepam	Long	5 mg	white scored tablet named BERK 1N4.
Somnite	Nitrazepam	Long	5 mg	white scored tablet with sailing boat on reverse.

Brand Name	Generic Name	Length of Action	Strength	Description
Nobrium	Medaze-pam	Long	5 mg	orange/ivory capsule marked ROCHE 5 in red.
			10 mg	orange/black capsule marked ROCHE 10 in red.
Anxon	Ketazolam	Long	15 mg	dark/light pink capsule in two sizes marked
			30 mg	ANXON with strength.
Centrax	Prazepam	Long	10 mg	blue scored tablet marked W and 10.
Xanax	Alprazolam	Medium	250 mcg	white oval scored tablet marked Upjohn 29.
			500 mcg	peach oval scored tablet marked Upjohn 55
Lexotan	Bromaze-pam	Medium	3 mg	pink hexagonal scored tablet marked L3
Noctamid	Lometaze-pam	Medium	500 mcg	white scored tablet with CG in hex.
			1 mg	white scored tablet with CF in hex.
Rohypnol	Flunitraze-pam	Long	1 mg	purple scored diamond-shaped tablet marked ROHYPNOL

List of Benzodiazepines available since limited prescribing

		Dose (mg) equivalent to 10 mgm diazepam
Chlordiazepoxide	Librium	25
Diazepam	Valium	10
Lorazapam	Ativan	1–2
Nitrazepam	Mogadon & others	10
Oxazepam	Serenid	20

		Dose (mg) equivalent to 10 mgm diazepam
Temazepam	Normison, Euhypnos	20
Triazolam	Halcion	0.5
Clobazam—may only be prescribed for epilepsy on NHS.	Frisium	20

NB: These dose equivalents are only approximate and adjustment to patients' individual requirements may be needed.

From the *Drug Newsletter* No. 31, April 1985.
Regional Drug Information Service, Newcastle upon Tyne.

FURTHER INFORMATION

Useful Tapes

Matthew Manning Cassettes Ltd., 39 Abbeygate Street, Bury St. Edmunds, Suffolk IP33 ILW
   Creative Visualisation: Fighting Back (for depression and relaxation);
   Fighting Addictions: Fighting Defective Eyesight: Fighting Insomnia: Fighting Allergies: Fighting Osteo-arthritis: Fighting Depression: Just Imagine: Just Relax.

Dr Claire Weekes, c/o Relaxation for Living, Dunesk, 29 Burwood Park Road, Walton-on-Thames, Surrey, KT12 5LH.
   Good Night, Good Morning: Moving to Freedom, Going on Holiday: Nervous Fatigue—Understanding and Coping with it: Hope and Help for your Nerves.

Muz Murray, Inner Garden Distributors, 30 Burton Avenue, North Walsham, Norfolk. NR28 0EP:
   Yoga Nidra

Further Reading

Martin L. Budd, *Low Blood Sugar* (Thorsons, 1981).
Dr Vernon Coleman, *Life Without Tranquillizers* (Piatkus, 1985)
Dr Wayne Dyer, *Your Erroneous Zones* (Sphere, 1977)

Celia Haddon, *Women and Tranquillizers* (Sheldon, 1984)

Alex Howard, *Finding a Way* (Gateway Books, 1985)

Ron Lacy and Shaun Woodward 'That's Life Survey on Tranquillizers' (BBC, 1985)

David Lewis, *Fight Your Phobia: And Win* (Sheldon, 1984)

Dr R. Mackarness, *A Little of What You Fancy* (Fontana, 1985)

Joy Melville, *The Tranquillizer Trap and How to Get Out of It* (Fontana, 1984)

Meg Patterson, *Hooked? NET: the New Approach to Drug Cure* (Faber & Faber, 1986)

John Powell, *Why Am I Afraid to Love* (Fontana, 1975)

——,*Why Am I Afraid to Tell You Who I Am?* (Fontana, 1975)

Release Publications, *Trouble With Tranquillizers*

Vicky Rippere, *The Allergy Problem* (Thorsons, 1983)

D. Rowe, *Depression: The Way Out of Your Prison* (Routledge, Kegan & Paul, 1983)

Robin Skynner and John Cleese, *Families and How to Survive Them* (Methuen, 1983)

David Smail, *Illusions and Reality: The Meaning of Anxiety* (J.M. Dent & Sons Ltd, 1984)

Dr Andrew Stanway, *Overcoming Depression* (Hamlyn, 1981)

Dr Claire Weekes, *Agoraphobia* (Angus & Robertson, 1977)

——, *Peace from Nervous Suffering* (Angus & Robertson, 1981)

——, *Self Help for Your Nerves* (Angus & Robertson, 1981)

——, *More Self Help for Your Nerves*, 1984)

Useful Reading for Professionals

'Benzodiazepine Withdrawal: An Unfinished Story', Heather Ashton DM, FRCP, *British Medical Journal,* Vol 288, 14 April 1984.

Dependence on Tranquillisers: Petursson & Lader, Oxford University Press, 1984.

'Effects of Benzodiazepines on Sleep and Wakefulness', T. Roth, F. Zorick, Jeanne Sicklesteel & E Stepanski. *British Journal of Pharmacology* (1981) 11, 31S–35S.

'Some Problems with Benzodiazepines', *Drug & Theraputics Bulletin* (Fortnightly for doctors from the publishers of *Which?*) Vol. 23 No. 6, 25 March, 1985.

'Lorazepam—A Benzodiazepine to Choose or Avoid?' *Drug & Theraputics Bulletin,* Vol. 23 No. 16, 12 August, 1985.

'Gynaecomastia & Diazepam Abuse'. Henning J. Moerck, Gerhard Magelund. *The Lancet* 23 June, 1979.

'Benzodiazepine Dependence & Withdrawal: The Problem', Drug Newsletter—Northern Regional Health Authority, April 1983.

'Benzodiazepine Dependence & Withdrawal—an update'. Drug Newsletter No. 31, April, 1985.

'Benzodiazepines in general practice: time for a decision', J. Catalan, D. H. Gath. *British Medical Journal,* Vol. 290, 11 May, 1985.

'Systematic Review of the Benzodiazepines', Committee on the Review of Medicines, *British Medical Journal,* 29 March, 1980.

'Rebound Insomnia—A New Clinical Syndrome', A. Kales, *Science,* Vol. 201, September 1978.

'Pills for personal problems', W.H. Trethewan, *British Medical Journal,* September, 1975.

'Nitrazepam (Mogadon) Dependence', P.C. Mistra, *British Journal of Psychiatry,* 1975, 126.

Useful Addresses

British Acupuncture Association, 34 Alderney Street, London, SW1V 4EU

National Institute of Medical Herbalists, P.O. Box 3, Winchester, SO22 6RB

British School of Osteopathy, 1–4 Suffolk Street, London, SW1Y 4HG

British Naturopathic and Osteopathic Association, 6 Netherhall Gardens, London, NW3 5RR

British Society of Nutritional Medicine, 9 Portland Road, East Grinstead, West Sussex, RH19 4EB

Pre-Menstrual Tension Advisory Service, P.O. Box 268, Hove, Sussex, BN3 1RW

British Society of Medical and Dental Hypnosis, 42 Links Road, Ashtead Surrey.

Relaxation for Living, Dunesk, 29 Burwood Park Road, Walton-on-Thames, Surrey, KT12 5LH.

Stresswatch (free advice—anxiety and phobic difficulties) P.O. Box 4AR London W1A 4AR. Send an $8\frac{1}{2} \times 4\frac{1}{2}$ inch S.A.E.

Yeast Infections
(Thrush – Chronic Candidiasis) in Withdrawal

It has been known for some time that antibiotics, steroids and the birth pill, weaken the immune system and allow organisms normally present in the body to get out of hand. This upsets the normal functioning of the body and causes a long list of physical and emotional symptoms. Evidence now shows that tranquillizers, and sleeping pills also, alter the normal flora of the gut and encourage the growth of candida. Treatment is effective and simple. It consists of diet, supplements (vitamins and minerals), and, for some, antifungal drugs.

Suggested reading:

Candida Albicans: Could Yeast be Your Problem, Leon Chaitow (Thorsons, 1985).

Nutritional Medicine, Dr Stephen Davies and Dr Alan Stewart (Pan, 1987).

INDEX

Of further interest . . .

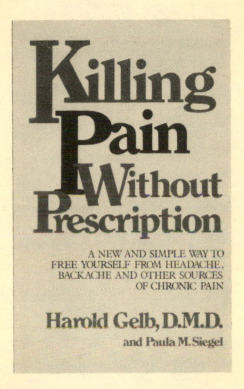

KILLING PAIN WITHOUT PRESCRIPTION

Dr Harold Gelb and Paula Siegel. A new multi-disciplinary approach to the treatment of pain, dealing with the three most prominent forms of chronic pain — neck, head and back. Pinpoints the TMJ syndrome as the most common cause. TMJ is the tempero-mandibular joint (jaw bone) and an imbalance here can affect the muscles in every part of the body. Dr Gelb combines theory, therapy and treatment from many medical disciplines into one sensible and complete programme for the chronic pain sufferer. *Includes:* biofeedback techniques; nutrition; hormonal balance.

ADDICTIONS

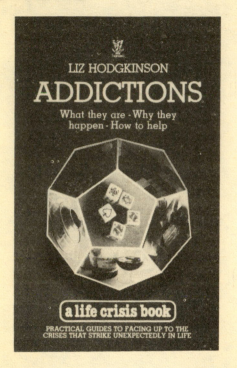

Liz Hodgkinson presents a down-to-earth guide for all those desperately trying to reach out to a loved one in the grip of some form of addiction. Gives compassionate yet accurate advice on the appeal of different substances, what they do to the user, how to recognise the warning signs and how to actually help. Areas covered include: alcohol; gambling, smoking; tranquillizers; bulima; violence, and drugs, with particular reference to heroin and the young. This excellent book also deals with the most recent of addictions—solvent abuse. *Includes actual case histories.*